ASSISTING DISPLACED WORKERS

Do the
STATES
have a better idea?

Duane E. Leigh

1989

W. E. UPJOHN INSTITUTE for Employment Research

Library of Congress Cataloging-in-Publication Data

Leigh, Duane E.
    Assisting displaced workers.

    Bibliography: p.
    Includes index.
    1. Unemployed—Government policy—United States—
States   2. Occupational retraining—United States—
States   I. Title.
HD5724.L3543 1989   362.85'0973   89-5844
ISBN 0-88099-073-2
ISBN 0-88099-074-0 (pbk.)

∞

ii

The Author

Duane E. Leigh is a professor of economics at Washington State University, Pullman, Washington. He earned his Ph.D. in economics from Michigan State University in 1969, and he has held teaching and research appointments at the University of Wisconsin—Madison and the University of Virginia. In addition to his work on displaced workers, he has published articles relating to racial differences in unemployment and labor force participation rates, factors leading to occupational advancement, union effects on wage and nonwage forms of worker compensation, and the determination of workers' preferences for union membership. He is also the author of a book titled, *An Analysis of the Determinants of Occupational Upgrading.*

Acknowledgments

The genesis of the research reported here was a contract awarded for the summer of 1986 by the Washington state legislature to study programs designed by other states to meet the adjustment assistance needs of displaced workers. Russell Lidman, director of the Washington State Institute for Public Policy, initiated the project, administered the contract, and provided direction for the research. Subsequently, financial support received from the W. E. Upjohn Institute for Employment Research allowed me to greatly expand the scope of the research, resulting in the present monograph.

A number of state officials and other individuals graciously supplied me with verbal descriptions and available written materials on particular displaced worker programs and demonstration projects. These individuals include

Susan R. Bass	Maryland Department of Economic and Employment Development
Kristine Coryell	Illinois Prairie State 2000 Authority
Richard D'Lorio	Rhode Island Department of Economic Development
Thomas L. Drabik	New Jersey Department of Labor
Sandra Glackin	California Employment Training Panel
Terry Johnson	Battelle Institute
Bonnie J. Lee	Arizona Department of Economic Security
Pam McCrea	Minnesota Department of Jobs and Training
Charles D. Smith	Massachusetts Division of Employment Security
Stephen A. Wandner	U.S. Department of Labor

The following friends and colleagues provided useful comments and criticisms on one or more chapters of the manuscript:

John Addison	University of South Carolina
Gary Bodeutsch	Washington State Employment Security Department
Daniel Hamermesh	Michigan State University
Ernst Stromsdorfer	Washington State University
Ronald Warren	University of Georgia
Larry Wohl	Gustavus Adolphus College
Steve Woodbury	Michigan State University and the Upjohn Institute

In addition, Lou Jacobson of the Upjohn Institute staff read the entire first draft and provided numerous suggestions that both sharpened the analysis and expanded its coverage.

Several other persons made valuable contributions to the preparation of the monograph. The research assistance of Tesa Stegner and Koushik Ghosh is much appreciated. Judy Gentry expeditiously handled the final steps of preparing the manuscript for publication. Finally, the importance of the love and encouragement of my wife, Joan, and our daughters, Brooke and Karin, cannot be overstated.

Contents

List of Tables

1
Introduction

It is widely recognized that in a dynamic, highly competitive economy, the displacement of workers from their jobs has been and continues to be an economic fact of life. An important source of this displacement during the postwar period has been the long-term shift in employment opportunities from manufacturing to services. Studies such as the report of the Secretary of Labor's Task Force on Economic Adjustment and Worker Dislocation (1986) suggest, nevertheless, that the extent of displacement among American workers may have increased in recent years. In support of its conclusion, the Task Force points to the dramatic increase in import penetration of U.S. markets; the rising proportion of permanent separations among total job losses during the 1981–82 recession relative to earlier postwar recessions; and the greater volatility since 1970 in exchange rates, interest rates, and energy prices. Stone and Sawhill (1987) document the incidence of difficult labor market adjustments arising from the increasing internationalization of the economy, and Hamermesh (1989) and Summers (1986) provide evidence indicating that the contribution of displaced workers to the nation's overall unemployment rate has recently risen.[1]

Displaced workers (also termed dislocated workers) are usually described as workers on layoff who possess a stable employment history with their predisplacement employer. In addition to their work experience, the main distinction between displaced workers and other laid-off workers is that the displaced typically have little chance of being recalled to jobs with their old employer or even in their old industry. At the time of layoff, however, displaced workers are likely to be unaware that their chances of recall are slim, although alternative employment opportunities exist elsewhere. The first step in the reemployment process is recognition of the need to engage in job search, followed

1

by a dusting off of job search skills which may have been unused for a number of years. Enhancing job search skills is important because of the very real possibility that a worker displaced by a major plant closure or mass layoff will face bleak reemployment prospects in his or her local labor market. Beyond gearing up for job search, it may also be necessary for some displaced workers to be retrained in the vocational skills required to qualify for jobs in expanding industries.

Displaced workers thus tend to differ from other unemployed workers in that the duration of their unemployment is likely to be longer and that their reemployment is likely to require a change in occupation or industry. Reemployment may involve as well a willingness to accept employment at a lower wage. In the words of the Secretary of Labor's Task Force report (1986:16), "[J]obs lost [by displaced workers] are often perceived as especially good jobs, for which the individual worked many years for one employer to achieve. Also, extraordinary emotional adjustments are required as life plans and goals are changed abruptly."

As experienced workers with stable work histories, displaced workers are usually eligible for unemployment insurance (UI) benefits. Indeed, the 26 weeks of income maintenance provided by UI in most states is often the only source of financial support available to them. The UI system has served for over 50 years as the first line of defense against temporary income losses due to unemployment. Nevertheless, a recurrent question about UI is whether income maintenance is the most appropriate form of assistance to individuals who have lost jobs in which they had substantial human capital investments and for whom prospects of obtaining reemployment using these skills are dim. Critics such as Kuttner (1985b), for example, argue that the funds used to pay UI benefits could be better spent on alternative programs designed to speed-up the reemployment of displaced workers. Reemployment programs discussed by Kuttner include retraining courses and wage subsidies intended to create new job opportunities.

At the federal level, the specific adjustment problems of displaced workers have been recognized in the Trade Adjustment Assistance program created in 1962 and 20 years later in the passage in 1982 of Title III of the Job Training Partnership Act. The reemployment programs funded by these laws are summarized in useful reports provided by the

U.S. Department of Labor (1986) and the Office of Technology Assessment (1986). More recently, President Reagan proposed, in the fall of 1987, a comprehensive program authorizing $980 million to be spent in retraining workers displaced by plant closings or technological change. This proposal became law in August 1988 as part of the Omnibus Trade and Competitiveness Act.

At the state level also, a variety of reemployment initiatives are currently in operation in virtually every state. These programs are generally funded by state general tax revenues, but three states—California, Delaware, and Washington—are financing their initiatives by special earmarked payroll taxes.[2] Under the Reagan administration, the evolving philosophy of new federalism has made the states the key intergovernmental actor in the areas of education, economic development, welfare, and employment and training. But despite the ingenuity, diversity, and substantial investment of resources in displaced worker programs, no comprehensive study of proposed and ongoing state initiatives is available at present. The purpose of this monograph is to provide a description and evaluation of state initiatives dealing with the problem of worker displacement. These initiatives include the provision of programs to retain jobs and encourage economic development, as well as reemployment assistance provided directly to workers in the form of retraining programs and job search workshops. The focus is on newer, more innovative state initiatives.

This chapter continues with an overview of some of the policy issues relating to worker displacement. Considered, in particular, are the questions of the incidence of displacement and whether government should be expected to provide displaced workers with special assistance (beyond or in place of UI). This section is followed by the introduction of half a dozen important questions which the monograph attempts to answer. The issue of how the various initiatives described in the study are to be evaluated is next considered. The chapter concludes with a brief description of how the remainder of the monograph is organized.

Displaced Workers: How Many and Should They Receive Special Assistance?

The Magnitude of the Problem

While it is fairly easy to describe in general terms how displaced workers differ from other unemployed workers, it is more difficult to pin down these distinctions with enough precision to permit an accurate quantitative estimate of the displaced worker population. Examples of the kinds of questions that must be answered in attempting to measure the number of displaced workers include the following:

1. How long must an unemployed worker have held the previous job to be counted as a displaced worker?

2. Can length of unemployment, UI eligibility, or even exhaustion of UI benefits be used as a criterion to distinguish displaced workers from other unemployed workers?

3. Must laid-off workers suffer a sizable decrease in wages upon reemployment to be counted as displaced?

4. Can displaced workers be distinguished from other laid-off workers by the reason for their layoff, or perhaps by whether the industry from which they were laid off is declining or particularly sensitive to increased foreign competition?

Since the answers to these and other questions can and do differ among analysts, it is to be expected that estimates of the displaced worker population will vary. This is indeed the case. But while there is no consensus in the literature on the number of displaced workers, there is agreement that the best source of data on displaced workers is the Displaced Worker Survey (DWS) first conducted by the Bureau of Labor Statistics as a supplement to the January 1984 Current Population Survey. A second DWS data set was made available to researchers in 1986. Both data sets are retrospective five-year surveys.

Flaim and Sehgal (1985) provide a benchmark analysis of 1984 DWS data. As described in their article, the DWS identifies a total of 13.9 million workers 20 years of age and older as being separated from their jobs over the January 1979 to January 1984 period. The data distinguish the following reasons for a job separation: (1) plant or company closed down or moved, (2) slack work, (3) position or shift abolished, and

(4) seasonal causes or other miscellaneous reasons not easily classified. Omitting workers on layoff for the fourth of these reasons, the estimated population of displaced workers drops to 11.5 million. Of these workers, Flaim and Sehgal note that a large proportion had been employed on their jobs for a relatively short time before they were laid off. Using three years of tenure as the cutoff point to distinguish displaced from other laid-off workers, the population of displaced workers falls to 5.1 million. It is worth noting that the number of displaced workers is quite sensitive to the specified years of tenure. A more liberal cutoff of two years would raise the count to 6.9 million, while a five-year cutoff would lower the estimate of displaced workers to 3.2 million.

Focusing on the Flaim-Sehgal estimate of 5.1 million displaced workers, table 1.1 identifies a number of the characteristics of these individuals. Displaced workers are seen to be primarily prime-age males who lost blue-collar jobs in manufacturing, especially durable goods manufacturing. Almost half of the 5.1 million reported that they lost their jobs because their plant or business closed or moved. An interesting finding is the number of workers who reported that they were not caught by surprise when they received notice of layoff. About 56 percent of all displaced workers indicated that they had received advance notice of their dismissal, or that they had expected it. Nevertheless, only about 11 percent of these workers left their employer before their job ended.

Table 1.1 also shows that more than two-thirds of the displaced workers drew UI benefits sometime during the five-year period covered by the survey, and that nearly half of the UI recipients were unemployed long enough to have exhausted their eligibility for benefits. Podgursky and Swaim (1987c) perform an econometric analysis of the duration of joblessness of DWS respondents displaced from full-time nonagricultural jobs between 1979 and 1981. Their results indicate that although nearly half of these workers found jobs within 14 weeks of displacement, there is a high risk that a displaced worker will experience a protracted period of joblessness. Especially noteworthy is their estimate that the probability an average male blue-collar worker displaced from his job would be jobless for more than one year exceeds 0.3.

Table 1.1
Summary Information on Displaced Workers
January 1979–January 1984

	Number[a] (thousands)	Percent
Total	**5,091**	
Age		
20–24 years	342	6.7
25–54 years	3,809	74.8
55–64 years	748	14.7
65 years and older	191	3.8
Sex		
Men	3,328	65.4
Women	1,763	34.6
Occupation of lost job		
Blue-collar	2,865	56.5
Other occupations	2,208	43.5
Industry of lost job		
Manufacturing	2,514	49.4
Durable goods	1,686	67.1
Nondurable goods	828	32.9
Other industries	2,577	50.6
Reason for job loss		
Plant closed or company closed		
down or moved	2,492	48.9
Slack work	1,970	38.7
Position or shift abolished	629	12.4
Notification of dismissal		
Received advance notice or		
expected layoff	2,870	56.4
Left before job ended	318	11.2
Did not leave before job ended	2,532	88.8
Did not receive advance notice		
or expect layoff	2,221	43.6
Received UI benefits	3,497	68.7
Exhausted benefits	1,670	47.8

Table 1.1 (continued)

	Number[a] (thousands)	Percent
End-period employment status		
Employed[b]	3,058	60.1
Full-time	2,266	79.7
Part-time	357	12.6
Self-employed	218	7.7
Unemployed	1,299	25.5
Not in labor force	733	14.4
Earnings relative to earnings on lost job[c]		
20% or more below	621	30.4
Below, but within 20%	320	15.7
Equal or above, but within 20%	571	27.9
20% or more	533	26.0
Loss of group health coverage[d]		
Employed	573	23.4
Unemployed	612	59.0
Not in labor force	196	40.3

SOURCE: Flaim and Sehgal (1985).

a. Subtotals may not sum to total.

b. Subtotals refer only to respondents who worked full-time in their lost job.

c. Includes only displaced full-time workers reemployed in full-time wage and salary jobs (N=2,045).

d. Percentages calculated in relation to number of respondents in each category who were covered by group health insurance on their lost job.

What was the labor market status of displaced workers at the end of the survey period? Table 1.1 indicates that 60 percent were reemployed as of January 1984, while about 26 percent were still unemployed and 14 percent had dropped out of the labor force (mainly into retirement). Focusing on the 3.1 million workers who were reemployed, about 2.8 million were full-time employees in their predisplacement jobs. Of these, about 80 percent were again employed full time at the end of the survey period, while 12 percent were holding part-time jobs and 8 percent were found in other types of employment (mainly self-employment).

Flaim and Sehgal point out that there are important differences by age, sex, and race in the proportions of displaced workers reemployed. In general, the younger the workers, the more likely they were to have obtained new jobs. Furthermore, displaced women were less likely than displaced men to have returned to work and were far more likely to have left the labor force. Finally, the proportions of black and Hispanic displaced workers reemployed (41.8 percent and 52.2 percent, respectively) were considerably lower than the proportion of whites (62.6 percent).

Another key finding concerns the number of displaced workers who moved to a new occupation or industry to obtain reemployment (not shown in table 1.1). Flaim and Sehgal (1985:10) point out, for example, that of the 980,000 reemployed workers who had lost jobs in durable goods manufacturing, only about 40 percent obtained reemployment in the same industry. Similarly, only about 35 percent of 493,000 workers were reemployed in nondurable goods manufacturing. Despite this evidence of substantial interindustry mobility, it is interesting to note that only a small minority of the 5.1 million displaced workers (680,000 individuals) moved to a different city or county to look for work or to take a new job.

The predisplacement and postdisplacement comparison of weekly earnings shown in table 1.1 provides additional information on the economic well-being of displaced workers who obtained new jobs by the end of the survey period. The table indicates considerable dispersion in relative earnings for workers reemployed in full-time wage and salary jobs, with 30 percent of workers suffering an earnings loss of 20 percent or more and another 26 percent of workers enjoying an increase in earnings in excess of 20 percent. In total, about 54 percent of reemployed workers landed on their feet in the sense that their new earnings equalled or exceeded their old earnings. This percentage is likely to be on the high side, however, since predisplacement earnings are not adjusted for the effects of inflation and increased labor productivity to make them comparable to postdisplacement earnings. It is almost a certainty, in addition, that displaced full-time workers who are reemployed in part-time jobs will suffer a sizable drop in earnings. Considering the situation of reemployed part-time as well as full-time workers, it appears reasonable to conclude that about one-half of the displaced workers reemployed in January 1984 were earning less than in their former jobs.[3] Also worth noting is the finding that nearly one-quarter of reemployed workers failed to regain the group health insurance coverage they enjoyed on their lost job.

During the fall of 1986, a second survey of displaced workers was released by the Bureau of Labor Statistics. As described by Horvath (1987), use of the Flaim-Sehgal criteria for distinguishing displaced workers from other laid-off workers resulted in exactly the same count of 5.1 million displaced individuals for the January 1981 to January 1986 period as for the 1979–84 period. Most of the conclusions drawn for the earlier period also hold for 1981–86. In particular, about half of the displaced workers had lost jobs in manufacturing, mostly in durable goods manufacturing; and about 55 percent reported that the reason for their job loss was a plant closing or business failure. As in the earlier period, the largest concentration of displaced workers was found in the heavily industrialized states of the Upper Midwest. More than half of those reemployed changed their broadly defined occupation.

The cyclical upswing in the economy during 1984–86 resulted in a higher reemployment rate of about 67 percent in 1986 compared to 60 percent in 1984, and a lower unemployment rate of 18 percent as compared to 26 percent in the earlier year. Nevertheless, the 1986 DWS indicates that there was little improvement in the proportion of displaced workers who were obliged to take a pay cut upon reemployment. For 1984, table 1.1 indicates that 46.1 percent of individuals working full time in both their predisplacement and postdisplacement jobs suffered a loss in earnings. The same statistic for 1986 is 44.1 percent. Over both five-year periods, about 30 percent of those reemployed in full-time wage and salary jobs suffered pay cuts of 20 percent or more. Levels of reemployment among older workers were still relatively low; in addition, reemployment rates for women, blacks, and Hispanics continued to fall considerably short of those for white males.

Should Displaced Workers Receive Special Assistance?

The very real possibility of large expected losses when a displaced worker suffers an extended period of unemployment or cannot find a new job offering a wage comparable to that earned earlier raises the issue of whether special assistance should be provided these individuals. The literature focuses on two reasons to explain why a displaced worker may suffer a substantial economic loss:[4]

1. The worker received an economic rent (i.e., a wage that is higher than his or her best alternative wage) on the last job. An example is the situation facing a worker displaced from a unionized job whose subsequent job is nonunion.

2. The worker invested in specific training on the last job in the expectation of a longer payout period than in fact occurred.

Concerning the first, there appears to be little justification for providing special assistance to workers who previously received above-equilibrium wages because they were sheltered from competition from other workers. The one argument supporting assistance in this case is that compensation may be needed to buy off politically powerful interests that would otherwise block socially desirable policies. A leading example of such a compensation scheme is the creation of the Trade Adjustment Assistance program in 1962 as a *quid pro quo* to organized labor in exchange for its acquiescence to trade liberalization (see Baldwin 1987).

The more important justification for special assistance to displaced workers is as a response to the loss of firm-specific human capital. Such specific skills include knowledge about the firm's operating procedures, the specialized products it produces, and its production and marketing arrangements. Although lost specific human capital cannot be replaced, assistance can still be justified in terms of both equity and economic efficiency. The equity explanation relates to the argument just made for compensating workers who have lost jobs which provided economic rents. The point is that since the nation as a whole gains from socially desirable policies such as free trade and the introduction of labor-saving technology, it is reasonable to extend assistance to those groups that bear the brunt of the adjustment costs associated with maintaining a dynamic, generally open domestic economy. Writing in *The Wall Street Journal*, Bhagwati (1988) argues that

> [O]pen markets cannot be sustained politically without institutions to soften the social impact of dramatic changes

resulting from foreign trade and investments. If better integration into the world economy means that large corporations can leave small communities and that changes in competition can result in social-adjustment problems, political prudence—if not humanity—requires that we help American workers cope with the consequences. . . . This is part of the grease that must be provided to let the wheel of capitalist fortune operate.

As noted in this quotation and emphasized by other authors including Bluestone and Harrison (1982, chap. 3), groups affected by social adjustment problems include not only displaced workers and their immediate families, but also the communities in which they reside.

The efficiency argument is that if losses due to displacement are uncompensated, risk-averse workers and their employers will be discouraged from investing in all forms of firm-specific human capital. The result of suboptimal investment in specific training is, in turn, a social loss due to an inefficient organization of production.

Hamermesh, Cordes, and Goldfarb (1987) make the further point that only workers whose loss of returns to specific training was unanticipated should receive special assistance. As they note, demand fluctuations occur frequently enough in some industries that periodic layoffs are a predictable aspect of employment. Hence job losses are likely to be anticipated by workers and compensated through the market in the form of a wage premium for the higher risk of a capital loss. Mass layoffs and plant closures, in contrast, are less frequent and thus less predictable. In the absence of predictability, job losses are more likely to be unanticipated, and workers at risk are less likely to receive compensation through the market.

The discussion of table 1.1 and the results of the second DWS indicate that job losses associated with plant closings and company relocations are indeed an important source of displacement, and that the movement between occupations and industries required to locate new jobs may well entail sizable losses of specific training. Econometric investigations of 1984 DWS data by Addison and Portugal (1987a), Madden (1988), and Podgursky and Swaim (1987b) provide evidence that a change in industry, in particular, entails dramatic decreases in earnings. Since union coverage is not reported in the DWS, however, it is difficult to distinguish whether the decrease in earnings associated with interindustry mobility represents loss of economic rents or loss of returns to specific human capital. Podgursky and Swaim deal with this data problem by merging information on industry unionization rates into their DWS sample. Controlling for industry unionization rates on the former job, the authors report for blue-collar males reemployed full time that a change in three-digit industry depresses earnings by 20 percent relative to the case in which a comparable displaced worker is reemployed in the same industry. A second commonly used measure of specific training—length of tenure on the predisplacement job—is also found to significantly increase earnings losses for blue-collar males.

Further evidence which helps to distinguish between the economic rent and specific human capital explanations is provided in an ingenious paper by Hamermesh (1987). Rather than comparing predisplacement and postdisplacement earnings, he uses the slope of estimated wage-tenure profiles to measure the extent to which plant closings are anticipated by workers. If the profile flattens out as the date of job loss approaches, the inference is that informed workers are responding to the decrease in expected returns by cutting back their investment in specific training.

Using the Panel Study of Income Dynamics data, Hamermesh's empirical results indicate that (1) displacement is not typically anticipated by workers and (2) earnings losses associated with unanticipated layoffs are quite large. Under reasonable assumptions about the real interest rate and the rate of depreciation of firm-specific human capital, he estimates that the present value of a worker's share of the lost returns on investments in firm-specific training is around $7,000 (in 1980 dollars). To this estimate must also be added the value of the often substantial periods of time displaced workers spend unemployed; the value of lost occupation- and industry-specific training; and the value of lost fringe benefits, particularly losses of unvested pension benefits and group health insurance coverage.

Major Questions to be Answered

While a case can and is being made that displaced workers are a population group deserving of special government assistance, several very practical issues immediately arise. What form should this assistance take? How should displaced worker programs be designed and put into place? Are there side effects of the programs which are unduly costly? And how should these programs be funded?

The perspective taken in this study is that state programs to assist displaced workers can be viewed as quasi-independent experiments whose designs and outcomes potentially offer a wealth of useful information to policymakers and labor market analysts. As will be described in detail, displaced worker programs range from conventional retraining and job search assistance programs to such unconventional initiatives as reemployment bonuses and unemployed entrepreneur programs. Controversial issues that arise in discussing the operation of these programs include "creaming" in the selection of program participants, the wisdom of tailoring programs to the specifications of particular employers, and the requirement that employers provide advance notice of plant closings and mass layoffs.

In formulating public policy, however, it is important to move beyond describing what has been tried to distilling what can be learned about how to best cope with the problems faced by displaced workers. Thus this study attempts to provide answers to the following major questions:

1. How do displaced workers differ from other unemployed workers?

2. Which forms of adjustment assistance "work" for displaced workers?

3. How should particular adjustment assistance services be provided?

4. What are the best time and place to provide assistance?

5. Is there a role for initiatives designed to keep existing plants open?

6. How should reemployment assistance to displaced workers be funded?

Evaluation Framework

An evaluation framework is clearly required to answer these and other related questions. Taking account of the twin objectives of raising postdisplacement wages and reducing the length of unnecessary delays in the reemployment process, the central policy question that must be dealt with in program evaluation is whether the stream of earnings available to program graduates is enough greater than their earnings stream would have been in the absence of the program to justify its cost. Ideally, as emphasized by Burtless and Orr (1986), evidence on this question would be obtained from a classical experiment in which the earnings of graduates are compared to the earnings of a control group, and assignment to both groups is made randomly. Random assignment is important because its absence is quite likely to mean that estimates of *net* program effects will be biased. (The net effect of a program is its effect on an outcome variable net of the change in the outcome variable that would have occurred in the program's absence.) For example, individuals who choose and are chosen to participate in a training program may be more highly motivated and job-ready than nonparticipants. If this is the case, a positive bias would be imparted to the estimated net program effect because the same unobservable characteristics that led to program participation also led to higher earnings. In the absence of a controlled experiment with random assignment, the nonexperimental approach to program evaluation focuses on differences in outcomes between program participants and an externally selected comparison group, and attempts to adjust statistically for the inherent differences between the two groups.[5]

Although controlled experiments with random assignment have been carried out for a few of the initiatives discussed in this study, information on individual program participants that would allow program evaluation of either the experimental or nonexperimental variety is not available for most state-funded initiatives. State legislators have generally not opted to devote scarce resources to funding the data collection effort required to conduct quantitative program evaluation. Rather, the data available for individual state programs typically are, at best, such summary statistics as placement rates, average postprogram earnings, and average cost per placement. In the absence of a control group, these summary statistics are of limited usefulness. With respect to postprogram placement, for example, the real issue is not the absolute level of the placement rate of program graduates but rather the placement rate for graduates as compared to the rate for a control group whose members did not have access to the program.

Given the number and variety of existing state programs and pilot projects, a three-level evaluation framework involving a mix of available quantitative and qualitative evidence is proposed. For any particular initiative, the first level is a consideration of existing quantitative evidence obtained using data on individual program participants and a control group of nonparticipants. A key example of an initiative for which experimental results are available is the reemployment bonus. The Illinois UI experiment and the New Jersey UI reemployment demonstration project examine the effectiveness of cash bonuses in speeding up the reemployment process.

If data allowing neither an experimental nor a nonexperimental approach to program evaluation are available (which is usually the case), the next level of analysis involves the use of quantitative evidence on similar kinds of programs provided by demonstration projects or pilot studies. Important sources of this type of evidence are federally-funded studies such as the Downriver project carried out over the 1980–83 period and the six-site Dislocated Worker Demonstration project conducted between October 1982 and September 1983.

If neither of the first two levels of the evaluation strategy can be applied, the final level is a type of qualitative analysis termed "process analysis." Rather than concentrating on program outcomes, process analysis focuses on how the program is operating as evaluated by staff members, participants, and outside observers. Some of the concerns addressed by this level of analysis include program design and implementation, selection of program participants and the allocation of services across participants, and occurrence of fundamental changes in the direction and funding of the program during its existence.

Organization of the Study

Chapter 2 focuses on state initiatives to upgrade the vocational skills of displaced workers through classroom and on-the-job training programs. Several issues relating to training programs are considered, and three state-funded programs are examined in detail. Also briefly discussed in this chapter are the efforts of the federal government over the past 25 years to improve the reemployment prospects of displaced workers.

In addition to classroom and on-the-job training, a third traditional type of assistance to displaced workers is designed to enhance job search skills. Chapter 3 describes the component services of a broadly defined job search assistance program and discusses the results from several demonstration projects that measure the net impact of this type of assistance. Also considered are the reemployment bonus experiments and two programs designed to test the effectiveness of more closely monitoring the search activity of UI claimants.

In chapter 4 the discussion shifts from different types of adjustment assistance initiatives to a consideration of the timing and location of program intervention. Specifically examined are (1) state laws requiring advance notification of planned plant closures or mass layoffs, (2) the new federal Worker Adjustment and Retraining Notification Act, and (3) state-level programs that deliver reemployment services on-site to displaced workers. A focal point of the discussion of on-site programs is the highly regarded Canadian Industrial Adjustment Service (IAS) program.

Chapter 5 includes a consideration of a number of other initiatives not yet discussed. These include state programs providing assistance to employee groups to save jobs by purchasing facilities that might otherwise close, enterprise zone proposals, and British and French initiatives to assist individual unemployed workers to start up their own small businesses. Also discussed in this chapter are several other initiatives which are part of the sweeping displaced worker program established by Massachusetts' Mature Industries Act.

Chapter 6 pulls together the results of the study by providing answers to the six key policy questions posed earlier. The chapter concludes with a consideration of what appears to be the best mix of programs to meet the needs of displaced workers.

NOTES

1. Using data for the 1968–81 period from the University of Michigan's Panel Study of Income Dynamics, Hamermesh finds that the rate of displacement (where displaced

workers are defined as those whose plants closed) showed a strong secular increase that is independent of the business cycle. Summers examines the rise in what he terms the "normal" unemployment rate over the past 20 years. He concludes that most of the additional unemployment is concentrated among mature men, job losers, and the long-term unemployed. The increased share of married women and young people in the labor force is found to have had essentially no effect.

2. Because UI trust funds cannot be used to pay for programs other than income maintenance, these state initiatives must be funded by earmarked payroll taxes or general state revenues. The funding of the California, Delaware, and Washington programs can be viewed as a diversion of UI tax revenues, however, since employers in these states had their regular UI payroll tax rates decreased at the same time that the earmarked payroll taxes were levied.

3. Flaim and Sehgal (1985:11) also emphasize that those displaced from high-wage industries are most likely to suffer a decrease in earnings upon reemployment. Among the 980,000 workers displaced from durable goods manufacturing, for example, median weekly earnings dropped by 21 percent from $344 to $273 in the jobs held in January 1984.

4. Madden (1987) considers a third explanation emphasizing that displaced workers encounter greater discrimination (or less favoritism) in the general labor market than on the last job. Using 1984 DWS data, she presents evidence indicating that women suffer a greater loss from displacement than men because sex discrimination in the labor market limits the job alternatives available to women.

5. An important controversy in the literature concerns the value of the nonexperimental approach to program evaluation. LaLonde (1986) and Fraker and Maynard (1987) provide evidence showing that nonexperimental strategies involving the selection of comparison groups from alternative data sources and the application of available econometric techniques fail to replicate experimentally generated results obtained by comparing the earnings of randomly assigned treatment and control group members. They therefore conclude that randomized experiments are necessary to reliably determine program effects. On the other hand, Heckman, Hotz, and Dabos (1987) argue that while in principle randomized experiments represent the most desirable approach to program evaluation, the actual implementation of experiments typically creates new forms of sample selection that require the application of nonexperimental econometric procedures for making statistical adjustments.

2
Vocational Training Programs

A traditional public policy remedy to prevent long-term unemployment is retraining—either classroom training programs or on-the-job training (OJT). The basic presumption of classroom training is that major groups of displaced workers lack the transferable skills that would permit them to become reemployed at comparable wages in their local labor markets. On the other hand, OJT is appropriate for displaced workers who possess the necessary transferable skills and aptitudes to adapt to the requirements of new jobs, but who lack firm-specific job skills.

For over 25 years, the federal government has offered vocational training programs to assist the unemployed to return to work. This chapter begins with a brief overview of federal job training programs, emphasizing those programs intended to provide assistance to displaced workers. Drawing on this background information, the next section discusses some of the difficult issues that arise in the provision of retraining assistance. Then, the operation of three state-funded retraining initiatives is examined in the context of these issues. The three state initiatives are the California Employment Training Panel, the Minnesota Employment and Economic Development program, and the Illinois Prairie State 2000 Authority.

A key policy issue relating to retraining programs is the question of whether or not they "work." Since the three state programs examined in this chapter were not designed with program evaluation in mind, the discussion draws mainly on the type of qualitative analysis described in chapter 1 as process analysis. Additional quantitative evidence on the effectiveness of retraining displaced workers is, however, available from a handful of federally funded demonstration projects. The concluding section of this chapter summarizes the results of the process analyses of the state programs considered and introduces some of the main findings obtained from relevant demonstration projects. As most of these demonstrations involve a comparison of the net impacts of classroom training, OJT, and job search assistance programs, the discussion of demonstration project results carries over into the next chapter, which deals with job search assistance.

Federally-Funded Programs

The federal government's first comprehensive attempt to assist displaced workers was the Manpower Development and Training Act (MDTA). Passed in 1962, MDTA represented the response of Congress to a rising national unemployment rate coupled with a growing concern over the effects of automation and technology on the employment options of mid-career adult workers. Originally funded at $100 million per year, the objective of the program was the retraining of unemployed individuals whose skills had been made obsolete by technological advancement. Retraining programs took the form of classroom training, OJT, and remedial education. By the mid-1960s, an improved labor market and lessened concern over automation led to a shift in interest and funding away from the employment problems of displaced workers and toward the employability of disadvantaged young people and welfare recipients. MDTA's emphasis on job training continued throughout the remainder of the 1960s and into the early 1970s, however.

In 1973, Congress created the Comprehensive Employment and Training Act (CETA), which consolidated nine earlier programs including MDTA. Two distinct types of programs were funded under CETA. Title I provided disadvantaged workers a program mix including classroom training, OJT, and "work experience" (subsidized public sector jobs emphasizing work habits and skill development). In contrast, Titles II and VI offered public service employment (PSE) programs to workers who had recently lost jobs in high-unemployment geographic areas. Title II was intended to serve the structurally unemployed, while Title VI was strictly a countercyclical job creation program. As unemployment rose during the 1970s, CETA expenditures shifted away from Title I training programs toward the provision of PSE jobs primarily funded under Title VI. PSE programs typically provided little or no formal training. Amendments to the CETA legislation in the late 1970s and early 1980s reduced PSE expenditures and finally eliminated PSE funding entirely.

Two other features of CETA are worth noting. First, the responsibility for running training programs was shifted from the federal government to local government units called "prime sponsors." Second, the U.S. Department of Labor (USDOL) funded, for the first time, the development of a longitudinal data base specifically designed for program evaluation. Barnow (1987) provides a useful survey of results of the major CETA evaluation studies.

In addition to MDTA, the other major federal program specifically intended to assist displaced workers was the Trade Adjustment Assistance (TAA) program. Also created in 1962, the objective of TAA was to provide income support and retraining to workers who lost jobs in industries adversely affected by foreign imports. For the first 12 years of the program, only about 35,000 workers received TAA assistance. This low rate of program participation reflected the stringent requirement that affected workers and firms demonstrate that trade liberalization led to increased imports which, in turn, were the *major* cause of reduced domestic sales and lost jobs. Most TAA participants were provided income maintenance support, with only about 10 percent receiving training, placement, or relocation assistance.

In 1974, Congress modified TAA requirements, making eligibility easier and providing a generous income support package. TAA support payments were allowed to supplement state UI payments during the period of UI eligibility (typically 26 weeks), raising them to a level of 70 percent of the previous weekly wage. In addition, benefits at that level were allowed to continue for an additional 26 weeks. If the worker was in a retraining program when the one-year period ended, moreover, TAA support could be continued for up to 26 more weeks. Thus TAA provided a maximum of 18 months of income support. With easier eligibility and improved benefits, TAA expenditures and the number of workers served increased rapidly over the next several years, peaking at $1.6 billion and 532,000 workers, respectively, in fiscal year 1980. Retraining, however, continued to receive relatively little attention.

New legislation passed in 1981 reversed the more liberal TAA requirements enacted seven years earlier. Eligibility was tightened, and income support was cut back to the level of UI payments (typically 50 percent of the previous weekly wage), with TAA payments allowed to begin only after exhaustion of UI eligibility. Under the new regulations, dollar outlays and number of recipients dropped substantially. Authorization for TAA lapsed in 1985, but legislation signed by President Reagan in April 1986 extended the program to the end of fiscal year 1991. The 1986 legislation includes a requirement that receipt of allowances is conditional on participation in a job search program, and that workers are to be encouraged, but not required, to enter a job training program.

The CETA program expired in 1982 with the economy in the trough of the deepest recession since the 1930s. Once again, the displacement of experienced adult workers became an important national issue. Rather than renewing CETA with its emphasis on public service employment, Congress enacted a broad new program—the Job Training Partnership Act (JTPA)—intended to train and place workers in private sector jobs.[1] The new law has three major titles. Title II provides training to disadvantaged youth and adults and summer jobs to disadvantaged youth. Title III funds training and other services for displaced workers. Under these two titles, federal dollars are allocated to the states, and the states are responsible for program design and implementation.[2] Finally, Title IV authorizes programs that are directly administered by the USDOL. These include training programs for native Americans, seasonal and migrant workers, and veterans. Federal appropriations from July 1984 to June 1985 for Titles II, III, and IV were, respectively, $2.7 billion, $221 million, and $800 million. By way of contrast, the budget for CETA in its peak year exceeded $9 billion.

Titles II and III of JTPA differ from CETA and earlier federal programs in several important respects:

1. JTPA puts strict limits on the share of funds that can be used to provide income maintenance for trainees. As noted, the TAA program provided very liberal income maintenance allowances to eligible unemployed workers. Similarly, the Office of Technology Assessment (1986:171) mentions that CETA was criticized for providing training

allowances that were higher than the wages trainees could earn in paid employment.

2. JTPA makes the direction of training programs the responsibility of state governors. Under Title II, federal funding to the states is reallocated by the governors to local units called "service delivery areas." With respect to Title III, governors more often have kept control over JTPA expenditures by designating an existing state agency to deliver services statewide or by appointing a state official to choose contract operators through competitive bidding. State control of JTPA programs allows for the possibility of substantial variation in the range and mix of services provided in response to interstate differences in economic conditions and the specific needs of the displaced worker population. Under CETA, in contrast, local prime sponsors reported directly to the USDOL.

One other significant organizational difference from earlier programs is that JTPA gives the business community, in the form of Private Industry Councils, an important share of the responsibility for designing and administering local programs. Each service delivery area is required to appoint a Private Industry Council.

3. JTPA requires each governor to issue performance standards for evaluating job training programs in the state. These performance standards may include financial awards to programs that exceed placement and participant cost criteria and sanctions against programs that fail to meet the standards.

Congress slashed the fiscal 1986 budget for the Title III of JTPA to about $96 million from $223 million in fiscal 1985. Title III funding for fiscal 1987 then rebounded to about $200 million. For fiscal 1988, President Reagan proposed a comprehensive program that would combine Title III with other dislocated worker programs including TAA. Under the new program, funding to provide displaced workers with retraining, job search assistance, and other forms of adjustment aid would nearly triple to $980 million from $344 million in fiscal year 1987. The Reagan proposal follows closely the recommendations of the Secretary of Labor's Task Force report (1986). As mentioned in chapter 1, the new program is now law as part of the Omnibus Trade and Competitiveness Act of 1988.

Issues in Providing Retraining Assistance

The 25 years of experience with federally-funded training programs has raised a number of issues to be considered in evaluating state-level initiatives. This section explores several of these issues before proceeding to a description of particular state programs.

What Is the Appropriate Mix of Services
for Displaced Workers?

Although displaced workers are by definition experienced adult workers, their reemployment assistance needs are likely to vary widely, reflecting differences in transferable skills and aptitudes and in local labor market conditions. Critics of JTPA suggest that Title III performance standards and the influence of the business community through Private Industry Councils may skew the mix of services offered to displaced workers. In particular, Title III program planners may pay too much attention to short-term placement rates and per participant program costs and too little attention to the longer-term objective of increasing participants' human capital.

To get a feel for the placement rates and per participant costs associated with various services, table 2.1 reports summary statistics for the six sites of the national Dislocated Worker Demonstration project. This federally-funded project was specifically intended to assess the effectiveness of alternative approaches to reemploying displaced workers. Across the six sites, over 10,000 workers enrolled in classroom training, OJT, and job search assistance programs. Corson, Maynard, and Wichita (1984:17) summarize the cost figures shown in the table, noting that for planning purposes average cost per participant ranges from about $400 to $1,000 for job search assistance, between $1,000 and $2,400 for OJT, and between $800 and $3,500 for classroom training.

Using the kind of information shown in table 2.1, JTPA critics suggest that inexpensive job search assistance will tend to be overemphasized while classroom vocational training will be underutilized because of its higher cost and lower immediate impact on placement rates. Similarly, remedial education programs would also be expected to be underutilized because of relatively low placement rates. A recent evaluation of

Table 2.1
Costs and Placement Rates, Dislocated Worker Demonstration Project, 1982-83

Type of service	Project site					
	Alameda	Buffalo	Lehigh Valley	Mid-Willamette Valley	Milwaukee	Yakima
Placement rate						
Job search assistance (JSA)	17.2%	62.4%	27.1%	68.0%	5.3%[a]	80.8%
JSA and OJT	32.4%	75.8%	47.5%	NA	87.0%	92.5%
Classroom training	16.5%	57.1%	38.9%	47.7%	[b]	46.7%
Cost per participant						
JSA	NA	$ 851	$407	$1,133	$ 73[a]	$1,387
OJT	NA	$2,319	$975	NA	$1,387	$2,481
Classroom training	NA	$2,431	$896	$ 802	[b]	$3,464

SOURCE: Corson, Maynard, and Wichita (1984).

a. Not comparable with other sites because the only JSA service offered in Milwaukee was job development.

b. Service not provided.

NA signifies "not available."

JTPA Title III programs by the U.S. General Accounting Office (1987a:46–47) reports that nearly all participants received some form of job search assistance, while about 26 percent of participants received classroom training. Only 6 percent of participants were provided remedial training, and such remedial training programs that were available averaged just two weeks in length. By way of contrast, the Office of Technology Assessment (OTA) report (1986:179) points out that a substantial minority of displaced workers—20 percent or more in some projects—are handicapped in finding new jobs because of serious deficiencies in basic reading and math skills.

While OJT programs tend to be more expensive than job search assistance, the virtual guarantee of immediate placement may also lead to an overutilization of OJT. Guaranteed placement occurs because the subsidy to employers providing training is typically contingent on the retention of trained workers for a period of 30 to 90 days.

How Are Program Participants to be Selected?

The same pressures on JTPA program planners to achieve high placement rates and low costs are also likely to affect their decisions in selecting trainees. The danger is that displaced workers most likely to be selected into training programs are those least in need of skill enhancement—a problem commonly known as "creaming." While some level of basic education and aptitude is necessary for retraining to be worthwhile, a case can be made that it is displaced workers at the low end of the skill distribution who should be first in line for access to retraining programs (see, for example, Blumenthal 1987). The U.S. General Accounting Office (1987a:39–45) reports that both older and less educated displaced workers are underrepresented in Title III programs. Using 1984 DWS data, only 8 percent of Title III enrollees were found to be 55 years of age or older, as compared to 20 percent of the displaced worker population. Similarly, 32 percent of all displaced workers had less than a high school education, whereas only 22 percent of Title III participants fell into this schooling category.

Another issue involving participant selection is income support for trainees. Since JTPA regulations discourage the provision of living allowances for trainees, the basic 26 weeks of UI is usually an essential part of the income-support package. The UI constraint has two effects on program operators. First, they are forced to set up worthwhile training programs that do not exceed the six months of benefits. This means that classroom training courses may have to be truncated or compressed in length to conform to the benefit period. Second, program operators are under some pressure to select program participants early in their period of UI eligibility to avoid foreclosing classroom training as an option to unemployed workers who have no other means of financial support.[3]

Forecasting Occupational Demand in Selecting Curricula

With reference to classroom vocational training, one of the most difficult tasks in the retraining process is to accurately forecast the occupational demand for labor so that curricula can be selected which supply marketable skills. Kulik, Smith, and Stromsdorfer (1984:30–38) provide a detailed discussion of the steps taken in the Downriver demonstration project to identify growth occupations and develop appropriate retraining programs. Most observers, however, question the usefulness of attempts to forecast occupational skill requirements. The OTA report (1986:201) notes that in many states good information, even about current openings in local labor markets, is unavailable.

Corson, Maynard, and Wichita (1984:16) also remark on this issue, drawing on the experience gained from the Dislocated Worker Demonstration project. They note that despite attempts to base course selection on area labor market data, many successful program graduates were unable to locate training-related jobs. Similarly, the report of the National Academy of Sciences' Panel on Technology and Employment concludes that there is little if any need for additional investment in forecasting occupational demand (see Cyert and Mowery 1987:142–43). In support of its conclusion, the Panel points to (1) the flexibility of the highly decentralized U.S. training system and (2) the low reliability of existing manpower forecasting models. Concerning the second point, the Panel notes that current forecasting models are weak methodologically and provide forecasts of a high degree of uncertainty.

JTPA's performance standards requirement allows program planners to shift to training vendors much of the burden of making sure that trainees acquire marketable skills. This shifting is accomplished through performance-based contracts. The initial decision on courses for classroom training is typically made by project planners with the approval of local Private Industry Councils. Then the training contract is put out for bids with the proviso that the training vendor must meet JTPA performance standards. Contracts often include the following types of performance standards:

1. A 75 percent placement rate for program graduates in full-time jobs, with all but 10 percent of the jobs being training-related.

2. A starting wage no lower than $4 to $5 per hour.

3. Retention of graduates on the job for at least 30 days.

Typical contracts require that these provisions be met before the training contractor is entitled to receive full payment.

The OTA report (1986:253) notes that reliance on performance-based contracting in JTPA programs appears to be growing. In a recent OTA telephone survey described in the report, about half of the states responding indicated that they make use of such contracts in their Title III programs, and 11 states indicated that they use them predominantly.

Should Employers be Paid to Provide Training?

JTPA regulations permit training contractors to be involved in selecting program participants and shaping curricula. Since contractors may be and often are private business firms, a creaming-related issue is whether public funds should be used to pay for training workers whom employers would have hired and trained anyway at their own expense. If this form of creaming should occur, the training program simply provides a windfall transfer from taxpayers to employers with no net benefit for targeted workers.

The employer windfall issue is put into even sharper focus when, as is often the case, the training contractors are large, profitable firms. In this situation, Blumenthal (1987) notes that some of JTPA's harshest critics label it "welfare for corporations."

State-Funded Training Programs

The recent USGAO report (1987a:2) points out that through June 1986 JTPA Title III programs assisted, at most, 7 percent of the estimated number of eligible displaced workers. This difference between perceived need and available federally-funded services represents a market niche that the states are attempting to fill. In his survey of state-funded training programs, Stevens (1986) reports that only six states do not commit funds to subsidize state initiatives offering classroom training or OJT.

State programs differ, in general, from comparable JTPA programs in at least the following two respects:

1. State programs are not exclusively targeted to specific groups such as displaced or disadvantaged workers. Rather, training is often made available to currently employed workers in order to avoid layoffs and plant closures.

2. Training is usually tailored to the needs of individual employers. This means that state training initiatives are viewed more as a tool for economic development than as an investment in human capital. That is, training programs have the demand-side objective of creating jobs as well as the traditional supply-side objective of raising the level of workers' skills to enable them to qualify for existing jobs.

Rather than attempting to provide a survey of all state-funded training programs along the lines of that furnished by Stevens (1986), this section focuses on the programs provided by three states. California's innovative program is selected because it is the largest and undoubtedly the best known state initiative. Even though it is not explicitly designed to upgrade workers' skills, Minnesota's program is considered next because it offers an interesting contrast to California in terms of both the type of subsidy and the characteristics of the population served. Finally, the training programs provided by Illinois are examined for three reasons. The first is the comprehensive nature of the state's approach to retraining, and the second is the use made of the state's existing educational infrastructure. Third, Illinois' Prairie State 2000 Authority is an interesting example of the recent emphasis of many industrial states on retaining rather than creating jobs.

California's Employment Training Panel (ETP)[4]

Begun in January 1983, California's ETP involves funding of $55 million per year to be used for retraining the following categories of workers:

1. Those who are unemployed and collecting UI benefits.
2. Former UI recipients who exhausted their UI eligibility within the past 12 months and are still unemployed.
3. Those who are currently employed but are likely to be laid off and claim UI benefits.

To qualify workers for retraining while still employed, employers must certify that in the absence of retraining, employees will be laid off and replaced by other workers who already possess the necessary skills.

The explicit objective of the Panel is to provide access to retraining for experienced workers who have been or are likely to be displaced from their jobs. In meeting this objective, one of the Panel's statutory responsibilities is to minimize the cost of UI by putting current recipients and exhaustees back to work and by preventing unemployment through retraining before workers are laid off. A second statutory responsibility is to foster economic development by helping to provide California employers with a skilled workforce.

Selection of program participants, curricula, and providers. To understand ETP's approach to retraining, it is essential to recognize at the outset that the program is almost entirely employer-driven. Training projects are typically initiated by a telephone call from an employer to one of ETP's regional offices. There are no application forms to fill out. A meeting usually follows in which representatives of the company and Panel staff members discuss an outline of the retraining project. The project will not be approved unless a specific employer has established a need for the program.

Retraining programs funded by ETP may be classroom training or OJT;[5] and the provider of the program may be either the employer requesting the training or an independent training institution such as a public or private school, a joint labor-management apprenticeship committee, or an employer association. Regardless of the provider, the employer selects trainees according to its own specifications (subject to the eligibility conditions listed above). Similarly, the employer sets the standards for successful program completion, and it must approve the training curricula if an outside training agency is used. In return for this discretion in all aspects of the retraining process, participating employers must make a good-faith commitment to hire or retain program graduates.

Following a meeting with the interested employer, ETP staff members develop an outline of the project which is submitted to the seven-member Panel for review. Representatives of the employer and the training provider (if the employer does not provide the training) appear at that meeting to explain the project. Once the outline is approved, the staff prepares a formal agreement for the Panel's approval at its next meeting. The formal agreement includes a negotiated fixed fee per trainee, and all contracting is done directly with employers or training agencies.[6] The Panel takes pride in noting that its staff, not the employer, does the paperwork, and that when speed is important the project outline and a formal agreement can be approved within a time period as short as one month.

Performance-based contracting. The previous section described the use of performance-based contracts in JTPA Title III programs, and noted that about half of the states enter into such contracts with training vendors. ETP's enabling legislation specifies an even higher level of accountability by requiring that all contracts between the Panel and employers and training agencies be performance-based. Moreover, a stringent definition of performance is applied. The full negotiated payment per person is withheld until trainees have completed their training programs, are placed in training-related jobs at wage rates stipulated in the contract, and are retained in those jobs for at least 90 days. In practice, training projects are typically not approved for jobs with starting wages of less than $5.00 per hour. Moreover, the jobs for which workers are trained must be good jobs in the sense that they offer long-term employment security and career potential. With respect to the withholding of full payment to contractors, only for nonprofit organizations is an exception made by allowing some advance and progress payments. For these organizations, 25 percent of the full payment is withheld until after the 90-day period. If all the trainees covered by the contract do not complete the 90-day employment period, the funds received for their training must be repaid to the Panel.

Summary statistics provided for the first four and one-half years of ETP are shown in table 2.2. Average cost per trainee on all projects ($2,515) is within the ranges noted earlier in connection with table 2.1 for classroom training and OJT. Also shown in table 2.2 are the same statistics broken down by target group. It is interesting to note that relative to programs that train only potentially displaced workers, programs that focus on the unemployed tend to have a higher average cost per trainee, a longer length of training, and a lower post-training wage. The 32 percent higher cost of training a new employee as opposed to retraining a current employee provides support for the Panel's philosophy of attempting to provide training prior to layoffs.

Table 2.2
Summary Statistics for the ETP Program, June 30, 1987

Type of project	Percentage of projects	Avg. cost/ trainee[a]	Post-training wage[b]	Avg. hours of training
All projects	—	$2,515	$8.35	329
Projects that train Unemployed only	27	3,135	6.47	503
Potentially displaced only	53	2,367	9.32	234
Both groups	20	2,459	8.24	333

SOURCE: ETP (1987, tables III–D and III–E).

a. Cost is for trainees hired in training-related jobs and retained in those jobs for 90 days.

b. Post-training wage for projects for which final billing and placement information is available. For other projects, wage is minimum stated in contract.

Placement rate information is also available as of June 30, 1986. Approximately 77 percent of all trainees successfully completed their training, and 83 percent of program graduates were placed in training-related jobs and were retained in those jobs for at least 90 days at a wage specified in the contract. Almost 94 percent of graduates found employment of some kind. These placement rates compare very favorably with those reported in table 2.1, although the absence of a control group and the possibility of creaming in the participant-selection process make comparisons of placement rates rather dubious.

Performance-based contracting was also used in the Buffalo and Alameda dislocated worker demonstration projects. While noting that this form of contracting has the advantage of increasing the likelihood of placement in training-related jobs, Corson, Maynard, and Wichita (1984:143–47) caution that contracting agencies should be prepared to assume several additional burdens. First, contract negotiators need to possess a detailed knowledge of specific costs in order to negotiate successfully. Second, the agency must have the capacity to monitor contractor processes and program outcomes. Third, the fixed costs of contract negotiation and monitoring should not be underestimated. In cases of inadequate contractor performance, finally, the agency, as an obligation to participants, may have to provide the promised services.

Funding. A unique feature of ETP is its funding mechanism. As noted in chapter 1, federal law prohibits states from using UI trust funds to pay directly the costs of training. To fund ETP, the California legislature therefore created a separate Employment Training Fund financed by a 0.1 percent payroll tax assessed on all employers with a positive reserve in their UI account. At the same time, California employers had their regular UI tax rates reduced by 0.1 percent. The funding of ETP can thus be viewed as a diversion of a small part of regular UI tax revenues to finance training and economic development. California was and continues to be in a favorable position to carry out this diversion because of a surplus in its UI trust fund. State law limits the amount of funds that can be placed in the Employment Training Fund to $55 million per year. Any remaining funds are deposited in the state's UI trust fund.

Since 1983, two states—Delaware and Washington—have followed California's example in establishing separate training and economic development funds financed by an employer payroll tax.[7] Delaware's experience differed from that of California, however, in that Delaware was initially deeply in debt to the federal UI loan fund. During the early 1980s, a federally imposed 0.6 percent penalty tax was levied on

Delaware employers to repay the state's trust fund indebtedness. When the debt was retired in 1984, employers received a 0.5 percent (rather than 0.6 percent) payroll tax reduction, with the incremental 0.1 percent dedicated to financing training and economic development programs. Revenues from the tax totaled $1.5 million in 1985. Twenty-five percent of the funds raised is for services contracted out through the Delaware Development Office, and the other 75 percent is used by Delaware's Private Industry Council to supplement its JTPA funds. The state's training program is directed toward the counseling, retraining, and placement of actively employed workers as well as displaced workers.[8]

The Claimant Placement Project approved by the Washington state legislature in 1985 as a two-year pilot project provides intensive job search assistance to UI claimants judged to be readily employable. The $4.6 million allocated to the pilot project (the program was scheduled to end on July 1, 1987) was obtained by diverting funds from the state's UI trust fund. Specifically, an earmarked tax of 0.02 percent was imposed on employer payrolls, with an offsetting reduction in UI tax rates of 0.02 percent for most employers. Like California, Washington was in a position to utilize the diversion approach to financing the new program because of a small UI trust fund surplus of $264 million (about 1 percent of the state's total wage bill). As will be described in more detail in chapter 3, a bill passed by the legislature in the spring of 1987 makes the Claimant Placement Project a permanent state program with funding provided by an earmarked 0.02 percent payroll tax.

Evaluation studies. The ETP program differs from the other state-funded programs described here in that it has been subjected to evaluation by outside agencies. In the first of these evaluation studies, the accounting firm of Arthur Young (1985) provides a descriptive analysis of the operation of the program through January 1985. Among the positive aspects noted in this study is ETP's flexibility and quick response time in meeting employers' requests and its high placement rate for program graduates. The study also comments favorably on the Panel's role in reducing UI costs and in encouraging employers to locate and expand in California.

The recommendations for improvement suggested in the Arthur Young study largely represent a fine-tuning of the Panel's operation and policies. These recommendations include the following:

1. The need for an improved information system for tracking the employment status of trainees.
2. The suggestion that the Panel establish program goals and priorities in making longer-term decisions about training programs.
3. The suggestion that the Panel review policies for determining whether workers are likely to be displaced and for calculating the fixed fee prices paid to contractors.
4. A need to review the appropriateness of Panel policies with regard to required minimum wages following the completion of training.

The second evaluation study is a quantitative analysis carried out by the Training Research Corporation (see Moore, Wilms, and Bolus 1988). Using data for 3,913 trainees enrolled in ETP programs between January 1, 1983 and December 31, 1985, this study investigates the impact of ETP on participants' annual earnings, their annual weeks of unemployment, and total UI payments. The analysis shows that, on average, annual earnings of unemployed workers who successfully completed the program increased by 76 percent from $9,628 to $16,912. In addition, their average annual weeks of unemployment fell by 56 percent from 6.2 weeks to 2.7 weeks.

These striking results should be viewed as preliminary in at least two respects. First, as noted in the Training Research Corporation report, there is no control group of nonparticipants against which to compare the record of ETP participants. Thus, for example, growth in the California economy over the period examined might have resulted in similar gains in earnings and decreases in unemployment for nonparticipants. Second, human capital theory leads to the expectation that a successful training program will result in higher wages for trainees. If the higher annual earnings are the result of lower unemployment or increased access to stable employment, however, the program's effect may have been to increase job search proficiency rather than to increase training-related skills. In this case, the benefits to society are less than the private benefits, since ETP participants may simply have taken jobs that otherwise would have gone to other workers. It is nevertheless interesting to note that ETP participants who were employed but potentially subject to displacement also experienced a sizable 27 percent increase in earnings.

ETP can also be examined in terms of the four issues raised earlier in this chapter in connection with federally-funded training programs. To briefly recapitulate, these issues involve (1) the appropriate mix of services, (2) selection of program participants, (3) forecasting occupational demand in selecting program curricula, and (4) subsidizing the training expenses of private employers. The strength of the ETP approach to retraining is that decisions on service mix and curricula are made by the market, not by program planners. As has been emphasized, a training program will not receive Panel approval unless a specific employer has asked for the program and committed itself to hiring program graduates. Entirely bypassed, therefore, is the problem that workers will be trained in skills that are no longer demanded by employers. In this connection, one of the recommendations in the Arthur Young report (1985:34) appears to miss the mark. The recommendation is that the Panel should use labor market data to set occupational and industry goals and priorities to be sure that program funds are spent in areas that will further the economic development of the state. One of the main advantages of the ETP approach is that such forecasting is unnecessary.[9]

Potential concerns about the program involve the issues of participant selection and subsidization of employers. With respect to the first issue, there is little question that adherence to a performance-based contracting system of compensating training agents encourages creaming in the recruiting and selection of program participants. One piece of evidence suggesting that creaming does in fact occur is the Panel's own finding that only 17 percent of Panel trainees had failed to complete at least 12 years of schooling (ETP 1987). The same statistic for the state's labor force as a whole is 27 percent. The report also points out that 23 percent of trainees were women, compared to a workforce that is 43 percent female. Blacks and Hispanics, nevertheless, are overrepresented among ETP trainees. In its early evaluation of ETP, the Arthur Young report (1985) also observes that the intensive screening of participants in entry-level programs contributed to what was viewed as the slow start-up of many ETP programs.

Moreover, ETP increasingly appears to be subsidizing training by employers of their current workforces as opposed to supplying training to unemployed workers. One reason, as noted in the study by the National Academy of Sciences' Panel, is that the requirement that trainees be placed in jobs for 90 days prior to payment to the training provider discourages many potential external providers, such as community colleges, from participating in the program (see Cyert and Mowery 1987:152). A consequence of the increasing retraining of the employed is that ETP may be substituting public funds for the training investments that employers would have made in the program's absence. This implies that there is little net increase in the delivery of training services to workers actually displaced from their jobs.

On the further assumption that large firms are better able to fund retraining than small firms, the following evidence on the size distribution of employers of program graduates is instructive (see ETP 1987: Table II-A):

Firm size	Panel trainees	Total state employment
0–49	18%	32%
50–99	6%	11%
100–249	10%	15%
250–499	14%	10%
500–1000	6%	9%
1000+	46%	23%

Firm size in this table is measured by number of employees. It is clear that ETP trainees are underrepresented in the workforces of small employers and overrepresented in the workforces of quite large employers.

In defense of ETP, at least three points may be brought out in connection with these concerns. First, it should be noted that a minimum level of general training is probably required before an individual can benefit from more specialized training, and ETP is specifically prohibited from offering remedial education. The continued active involvement of employers is likely to be conditional on a high degree of assurance that program graduates will be able to perform successfully in the jobs they have been trained for without the need for supplemental OJT.

Second, the year 1987 marked an important transition for ETP in that, for the first time, employers' demand for training assistance exceeded the supply of available funds forcing the rationing of funds among prospective contractors. This excess-demand situation has led the Panel to impose certain priorities on its basic system of responding to the market demand for training. In particular, the list of Panel priorities includes expedited consideration given to proposals in which special employment opportunities are offered to minorities, women, the disabled, and veterans and to proposals which promise assistance to persons already laid off or in danger of layoff due to plant closures or permanent mass layoffs. In addition, the Panel has committed itself to targeting approximately 30 percent of its funds for projects retraining the unemployed; and it is conducting a special marketing outreach to small businesses and minority- and female-owned enterprises.

Finally and most fundamentally, ETP should be properly viewed as an economic devleopment program to assist both employers and workers as opposed to a jobs program to assist disadvantaged workers. From this perspective, a major goal of the program is to provide employers with an incentive to modernize plants and avoid layoffs by subsidizing the costs of retraining existing employees. With respect to subsidizing the training expenses of large employers, it should be pointed out that large firms provide jobs that pay high wages and offer career potential— that is, the kinds of jobs that are mandated by ETP's enabling legislation. Since ETP is funded by what amounts to a portion of the UI payroll tax, moreover, political support for the program is strengthened if every employer who pays UI taxes, regardless of size, is permitted to benefit. In this regard, a *BusinessWeek* (1985) article quotes a Bank of America official as stating that an ETP-funded training program allowed the bank a return on its UI tax payments that it would otherwise not have received because of its negligible layoff rate.[10] As will be described in the next section, Minnesota's MEED program takes the opposite approach of giving small employers priority in program participation.

The Minnesota Employment and Economic Development (MEED) Wage-Subsidy Program

MEED design and implementation. Originally titled the Minnesota Emergency Employment Development Program, MEED was created under circumstances quite different from the ETP program. In the case of ETP, California officials were required by statute to lower their UI payroll tax rate because of the large UI trust fund surplus that had accumulated. Resources were thus made available to initiate a new program at no additional cost to state taxpayers. In contrast, MEED was created in 1983 by a Minnesota state legislature faced with double-digit unemployment rates coupled with a high percentage of unemployed workers who had exhausted their UI eligibility. The legislature's response in MEED was a two-year program designed to create temporary jobs in the public sector and permanent jobs in the private sector. The program was initially funded at a hefty $70 million for the July 1983–June 1985 biennium using general tax revenues.

As originally conceived, MEED was fundamentally an emergency job creation program, with at least 60 percent of the created jobs expected to be in the public sector. The focus on public sector job creation was due to the legislature's initial skepticism about the willingness of private sector employers to participate in MEED. As the program evolved, however, greater than expected participation of private sector employers led to a reversal in job placement objectives. By the second year of the program, 60 percent of jobs were designated to be in the private sector (a 70 percent private sector placement rate was actually achieved); and an additional $30 million was appropriated by the legislature. MEED was made a permanent program in 1985. Currently, a minimum of 75 percent of jobs created must be in the private sector;[11] and $27 million was appropriated for MEED for the biennium ending June 30, 1987. It is worth emphasizing that Minnesota continues to devote substantial resources to MEED, even though the economic crisis that led to its creation is past.

The private sector component of MEED is a wage-subsidy program. Specific features of the wage-subsidy are the following:

1. Eligible job seekers are those who are unemployed and are ineligible for or have exhausted either UI benefits or workers'compensation. Prior-

ity is given to applicants living in households with no other source of income, to those eligible for general assistance, to those eligible for Aid to Families with Dependent Children (AFDC), and to farm families that can demonstrate severe financial need. MEED is therefore available to assist displaced workers who have exhausted their UI eligibility, but it is not restricted to only displaced workers.

2. MEED offers employers who hire targeted workers a subsidy of up to $4 per hour in wages and up to $1 per hour in fringe benefits for a period not to exceed six months. The six-month period can be extended up to one year for workers undergoing job training. A worker's wage is set by the employer and must be equal to the wage paid other employees for the same work.

3. Participating employers are given an incentive to retain targeted workers for at least 12 months beyond the six months of subsidized employment. Employers are required to repay 70 percent of the amount received under the program if the employee is not continued on the job beyond the initial six months. No repayment is expected, on the other hand, if targeted workers are retained one year or longer beyond the subsidy period. A prorated portion of the subsidy must be repaid for employees retained less than one year. Employers are also prohibited from laying off or reducing the hours of other employees in order to hire subsidized workers.

4. Given priority for MEED participation are small businesses as well as firms that offer the potential for long-term employment, that conserve energy, that make use of state resources and new technology, that operate primarily in Minnesota, and that are female- or minority-owned.

The MEED annual report (1987) covering the July 1985 to December 1986 period indicates that 85 percent of private sector participants were employed in unsubsidized jobs at the time of a 60-day follow-up survey after the completion of the subsidy period. Of those workers in unsubsidized jobs, nearly 91 percent were still employed by the same firm, while about 9 percent changed employers following the subsidy period. Average unsubsidized hourly wages for the two groups were $5.37 and $6.06, respectively. Most individuals employed under MEED qualify for the full subsidy over 26 weeks. Hence, average program cost per worker is relatively high at approximately $4,680.

Contrasts with ETP. Beyond the difference in economic circumstances existing at their creation, the MEED program offers an interesting contrast to California's ETP in three additional respects. One contrast is in underlying philosophies. ETP's philosophy is that updated skills are a prerequisite for workers to obtain or retain jobs. Thus payments made to employers providing OJT are viewed as compensation for training costs. In contrast, the explicit philosophy of MEED is that job seekers need employment, not retraining. If jobs are available, workers will be found to fill them. From this perspective, wage-subsidies are primarily viewed as a job creation device. Nevertheless, MEED-funded jobs do appear in many cases to offer training opportunities. A survey carried out by a coalition of state organizations, the Jobs Now Coalition, indicates that over 77 percent of participating private sector employers provided an affirmative answer to the question, "Did you provide any special training on- or off-the-job?" (See Rangan 1985.)

A second difference between the programs concerns the characteristics of workers likely to receive assistance. The earlier discussion of ETP suggests that creaming is likely to be involved in the trainee-selection process. MEED, on the other hand, targets the wage-subsidy to members of specific disadvantaged groups. A more recent 1987 Jobs Now Coalition survey (see Rode 1988) indicates, in fact, that MEED placements are disproportionately held by general assistance eligibles, women, and minorities. Fifty-four percent of its placements during the 1985–87 biennium were general assistance eligible, 42 percent were women, and 25 percent were minorities (in a state with a total minority population of only 4 to 5 percent).

A final difference is in the mix of participating employers. As noted, relatively large California employers are more likely than smaller employers to participate in ETP. In line with MEED's legislative priorities, on the other hand, small Minnesota employers are heavily involved in the program. The 1987 Jobs Now Coalition survey reports the following information on the size distribution of participating employers (see Rode 1988:Table 5):

Firm size	Participating firms
Less than 20	81.1%
21–50	9.7%
51–99	4.8%
100 or more	4.3%

where firm size is again measured by number of employees. As large firms are known to pay higher wages on average than smaller firms, the MEED wage-subsidy represents an especially large cut in labor costs to smaller firms.

Contrast with the Dayton wage-subsidy experiment. It is also interesting to contrast the experience of the MEED program to date with the results of a federally-funded controlled experiment carried out in Dayton, Ohio during 1980 and 1981. As described by Burtless (1985), the purpose of the Dayton experiment was to test the effectiveness of a targeted wage-subsidy program in increasing the labor market success of disadvantaged workers. Program-targeted workers, who were all AFDC or general assistance recipients, were randomly assigned to one of three groups. The first group of workers received vouchers that entitled their employers, upon making a hiring commitment, to a tax credit equal to 50 percent of earnings paid during the first year of employment and 25 percent of second-year earnings. Rather than a tax credit, the vouchers received by the second group authorized their employers to receive direct cash payments equal to the same percentages of first- and second-year earnings. Subsidy limits for both treatment groups were $3,000 and $1,500, respectively, for the first two years of employment. The third group of targeted workers served as the control group and received no vouchers. Members of all three groups received two weeks of job search training, which were followed by six weeks of structured job search. The vouchers expired at the end of the six-week job search period.

The Dayton experiment was designed to address two specific research issues. The first was to determine whether giving job seekers themselves the responsibility of informing prospective employers of their eligibility for subsidy benefits would increase the low take-up rates that have historically plagued targeted wage-subsidy programs. The second was the question whether firms with no tax liabilities to be reduced by a tax credit (because their profits are low or they are suffering losses) can still be induced to hire disadvantaged workers with the promise of direct cash payments.

The results of the experiment were unexpected. Among the two treatment groups, 13.0 percent of the tax credit group and 12.7 percent of the direct cash payment group found employment during the eight weeks of the experiment. Thus the direct cash payments did not increase labor market success relative to the tax credits. More important, the placement rates of both treatment groups were *lower* than the 20.6 percent rate obtained by the control group. Unfortunately, the evaluation of the experiment is limited to an analysis of placement rates and initial wages because of its premature cancellation in the spring of 1981. (There was essentially no difference in average wages between the treatment groups and the control group.) Subject to this qualification, Burtless interprets the results as indicating that employers used the vouchers primarily as a labor market signal of potentially poor job performance. This explanation would account for both the lower placement rates observed for the treatment groups and the failure of the different subsidy payment mechanisms to make a difference. The disquieting implication for current and proposed wage-subsidy policies is that vouchers have a stigmatizing effect in the sense that rather than easing the placement of target groups, the vouchers provide information which employers used to discriminate against the disadvantaged.

In contrast to the Dayton experiment, the MEED wage-subsidy appears to have been enthusiastically received by Minnesota employers, particularly small and relatively new businesses, despite the priority given to hiring hard-to-employ target groups. This is indicated by the shift in the program's emphasis toward private sector job creation, its continued funding during the economic recovery following the 1981–82 recession, and surveys describing a high degree of employer satisfaction with MEED. The reasons for the difference in employers' reactions to the two programs can only be speculated upon. Nevertheless, it is clear that MEED officials, like those of California's ETP program, recognize that it is critical to retain the support of the business community. From this perspective, the following considerations may play a role in MEED's relative success.

1. MEED is promoted as a program to assist Minnesota's small businesses to grow and diversify. In other words, MEED is sold as an economic development tool rather than as a program to assist the unemployed and disadvantaged. In this connection, the 1987 Jobs Now Coalition survey (see Rode 1988) points out that 81 percent of surveyed employers responded affirmatively to a question that asked whether

MEED enabled them to expand their production or scale of operations, 60 percent noted that the subsidy made it possible for them to invest in new capital equipment, and 54 percent stated that MEED made it possible to diversify into new areas. Among firms that reported expansion of their workforces, 56 percent indicated that they would not have been able to create new jobs without MEED assistance, and another 4 percent suggested that their expansion would have been delayed without the program. A further breakdown of these data suggests that MEED assistance is particularly beneficial to the growth of very small and new businesses. The same survey indicates, finally, that 86 percent of responding employers responded that they were "very satisfied" with their MEED employees, and only 23 percent mentioned that the subsidy failed to improve the performance of their business.

2. MEED officials have taken pains to keep their rules simple and administrative overhead low. The 1987 Jobs Now Coalition survey reports that 92 percent of responding employers felt that they were able to fill their jobs with a minimum of red tape, and 94 percent stated that they found the rules easy to understand.

As noted at the beginning of this section, most state-funded training programs pose few constraints on employers in their selection of trainees. The MEED program demonstrates that it is possible to walk the fine line between targeting assistance to particular groups of workers while at the same time enjoying widespread business support.[12]

Illinois' Retraining Programs

Illinois is unique among the states in offering a comprehensive three-pronged approach to retraining. The Illinois programs are (1) the Industrial Training Program authorized in 1979; (2) the High Impact Training Services program created in 1985; and (3) the Prairie State 2000 Authority, also created in 1985. The Prairie State 2000 Authority is emphasized in this discussion because it is representative of the recent focus by some states on retraining programs intended to retain rather than to create jobs.

The Industrial Training and High Impact Training Services Programs. Administered by the Illinois Department of Commerce and Community Affairs, the Industrial Training Program provides cost-sharing for

the OJT expenses incurred by "new" or "expanding" industrial enterprises. Expansion is defined in the enabling legislation as "a permanent increase in production that results in the addition of personnel
through additional work shifts and/or facilities in excess of normal growth
or turnover." Just what constitutes normal growth or turnover is not
spelled out. The program's contribution to the costs of OJT cannot exceed two-thirds of direct costs unless the trainees are unemployed, receiving state welfare benefits, or enrolled in training for the handicapped.
For each of these categories of trainees, the Industrial Training Program is authorized to provide up to 100 percent of training costs.

Emphasizing classroom training rather than OJT, the High Impact
Training Services program is also administered by an existing state agency—in this case, the Illinois State Board of Education. This program is
intended to provide an economic development role for the state's
vocational-technical education facilities. Private sector employers interested in program funding must join with a community college, area
vocational center, or comprehensive high school in putting together a
collaborative proposal. These joint proposals are then submitted to the
state Board of Education, which is obligated to respond promptly with a
decision on funding. As is the case for the Industrial Training Program,
program participation is restricted to new and expanding enterprises.

The High Impact Training Services program is similar to
Massachusetts' Bay State Skills Corporation (BSSC) in attempting to
establish cooperative relationships between employers and state educational institutions. Begun in 1981, the BSSC encourages educational
institutions and other training agencies to propose new courses and programs that are directly responsive to the demands of the marketplace.
But the BSSC will only fund proposals identifying one or more companies that will participate directly in the training. Participating firms
are required to match at least 20 percent of BSSC funds with direct
or in-kind support.

The Prairie State 2000 Authority. In contrast to the first two Illinois
programs with their job-creation emphasis, the primary mission of the
Prairie State 2000 Authority is to *retain* jobs already located in the state.
Job retention is accomplished by upgrading the skills of Illinois workers
so that they can adapt to advances in technology and other changes in

the workplace. With its focus on retaining jobs, the 2000 Authority is similar to retraining programs offered by such Upper Midwest states as Michigan and Ohio. The programs in both of these states are primarily intended to make use of existing systems of vocational and technical schools and community colleges to provide skill upgrading.

The Illinois state legislature initially created the Prairie State 2000 Fund in 1983 with the objective of assisting UI recipients and employed workers at risk of layoff to retrain themselves to meet the skill requirements imposed by technological change. The program did not receive state funding, however, until the passage of an amendment in 1985 creating the Prairie State 2000 Authority as an independent state agency.[13] The 2000 Authority has the following two components: the Individual Training Assistance Program and the Employer Training Assistance Program. In the Individual Training Assistance Program, the 2000 Authority issues training vouchers to approved training institutions (community colleges, school districts, and not-for-profit organizations) on behalf of individual trainees. Upon the enrollment of a trainee, the participating institution is permitted to redeem a voucher to cover the individual's tuition and related fees. Vouchers are valued at up to $2,000 for eligible unemployed persons and up to $1,000 for eligible employed individuals. Eligibility criteria are quite minimal. Unemployed applicants must have worked a minimum of three years out of the past ten in UI-covered employment, and employed applicants must be in need of additional skills to retain their present jobs. It is the responsibility of each participating educational institution to admit trainees and to assign each trainee an appropriate training curriculum.

The more important component of the 2000 Authority is the Employer Training Assistance Program which provides qualifying employers with a loan or grant to cover the direct costs of supplying training. Of the agency's fiscal 1987 budget of $3 million, about 87 percent was spent on grants and loans under the employer assistance program. The loan option covers 100 percent of direct training costs, and 25 percent of the principal of the loan is forgiven if trainees are retained by the employer for one year. The grant option covers 50 percent of direct training costs, with half the grant amount dispersed in advance of training and the other half paid after trainees are retained on the job 90 days from completion of training. A third funding option is to couple a grant request covering 50 percent of allowable training costs with a loan request to cover the remaining 50 percent. In general, funding approval is based on a demonstration that the training cannot be internally financed by the employer and that workers are in jeopardy of being laid off unless additional training is made available to them.

Evidence related to the retraining vouchers provided by the Individual Training Assistance Program is available from the income maintenance experiments carred out between 1970 and 1978 in Seattle and Denver (the SIME/DIME experiments). All experimental subjects were eligible for free employment counseling, and a subset of subjects was eligible for a training subsidy at the rate of either 50 percent or 100 percent of direct costs incurred. The training subsidy program operated like a voucher system in that the training provider and the curriculum chosen were left up to the individual.

A study of the training subsidy program by Hall (1980) indicates that participation was far short of universal. The participation rate for the counseling treatment was 42 percent, while 22 percent and 35 percent of those eligible for the 50 and 100 percent training subsidies, respectively, chose to enroll in a training program (mainly courses provided by community colleges). Concerning postprogram wage rates, Hall tentatively concludes that while the point estimates indicate a small positive training effect, the size of the associated standard errors make it impossible to reject the null hypothesis that the effect is zero.

A secondary mission of the 2000 Authority is to investigate innovative employment programs. In this capacity, the agency is planning a four-year pilot project to examine the feasibility of Individual Training Account (ITA) programs in Illinois. The basic idea of the ITA concept is to provide a fund privately financed by workers, employers, or both workers and employers that can be drawn upon to pay for additional educational or training investments. Choate and Carey (1985) and Lovell (1984) have presented specific proposals for implementing the ITA concept.

In the Choate-Carey proposal, contributions by both workers and employers would be used to create an ITA trust fund. A worker displaced from his or her job would be entitled to receive a voucher valued at up to $4,000 to be used to pay for retraining and/or relocation. If the retraining option were chosen, the type and location of training would be left up to the worker. At the time of retirement, both workers and employers would be refunded their unused contributions plus interest. The Lovell proposal differs in that displaced workers who choose to participate in the program would first be provided several weeks of counseling and job search assistance. If these services do not result in a satisfactory job placement, the participant is then given a voucher to pay for a retraining program of his or her choice. With respect to both ITA proposals, the OTA report (1986:267) makes the useful observation that the training voucher system would serve best to encourage lifetime education and retraining, as opposed to a crisis response to the specific needs of displaced workers.

Summary

In the context of the experience gained from over 25 years of federally funded vocational training programs, this chapter described the innovative state-level training programs in California, Minnesota, and Illinois. State training initiatives tend to differ from federal programs in terms of their availability to employed workers at risk of being displaced and their important economic development role. As an economic development tool, state initiatives have the demand-side objective of creating jobs as well as the traditional supply-side objective of increasing workers' human capital.

Begun in 1983, California's ETP program is the largest and best known of state-funded training initiatives. Among the innovative features of ETP are the following: (1) the heavy involvement of employers in designing individual projects and choosing trainees and program providers (in the case of classroom training), (2) the commitment required of participating employers to hire program graduates, (3) the high level of accountability imposed on training providers by the use of performance-based contracts, and (4) the diversion of UI tax revenues to fund the costs of training programs.

The Minnesota MEED program was created in 1983 as a temporary job creation program mainly directed toward jobs in the public sector. Originally conceived as a temporary two-year program, the unexpectedly favorable response of private sector employers to MEED led to its continuation as a permanent program emphasizing private sector job creation. The private sector component of MEED provides a targeted wage-subsidy to employers. Three features of the program are especially noteworthy. First, in contrast to most state programs, MEED is targeted toward specific groups of hard-to-employ persons. Second, despite questions raised in the literature about employers' interest in participating in targeted wage-subsidy programs, MEED is strongly supported by Minnesota businessmen, especially the small business community. Finally, MEED appears to be having a positive impact on skill upgrading although it is primarily promoted as an economic development tool.

The final state program considered—Illinois' Prairie State 2000 Authority—was examined because it is representative of the recent emphasis in heavily industrial states on retraining programs intended to retain rather than to create jobs. The 2000 Authority has two component programs. In the first, individuals in need of retraining are assisted through the provision of vouchers to be used at approved training institutions. In the more important second component, employers seeking to upgrade the skills of their workers are provided grants and/or loans to cover the direct costs of providing retraining services.

Process analyses of the California and Minnesota programs indicate generally favorable results, particularly as viewed as an economic development tool. As noted in the introductory section, however, neither ETP nor MEED was designed to allow program evaluation involving a control group comparison. The available quantitative evidence for assessing the net impact of retraining programs comes mainly from federally-funded demonstration projects, and this evidence indicates a less favorable view of the effectiveness of retraining.

Two of the most influential of these federally-funded demonstrations are the Downriver dislocated worker project and the Dislocated Worker Demonstration project. Carried out between 1980 and 1983 in the Detroit metropolitan area, the Downriver project provided a full range of reemployment services (i.e., classroom training, OJT, and job search assistance) to about 2,100 workers displaced from their jobs due to the closure of several auto assembly and auto parts plants. The evaluation report by Kulik, Smith, and Stromsdorfer (1984) points out that the Downriver project significantly increased participants' access to training opportunities over what would have been expected in the program's absence. Despite the increased access to training opportunities, however, the authors find that retraining does not yield a statistically significant incremental gain in participants' reemployment experience above that resulting from job search assistance (JSA) only. Average training costs per participant were more than twice the average costs of JSA.

The Downriver project was followed in 1982 by the Dislocated Worker Demonstration project, which was carried out to test the effectiveness of alternative reemployment services under a wider range of operating conditions. Although all six sites of the project offered displaced workers a full range of reemployment services, the Buffalo program was selected for a full impact study mainly because its evaluation design offered the best opportunity for estimating net program impacts.

In their evaluation of the Buffalo project, Corson, Long, and Maynard (1985) draw four important conclusions regarding retraining programs. First, less than 20 percent of the displaced workers recruited for the program chose to participate. The recruitment of more recently laid-off workers appears to lead to higher overall participation rates. Second, program participation had large and statistically significant effects on reemployment and average weekly earnings. Third, both classroom training and JSA significantly facilitated worker readjustment, with the estimated impacts being of similar size. Given its substantially lower cost ($851 per participant versus $2,431 per participant for classroom training), the absence of an incremental impact for classroom training suggests that JSA is the more cost effective of the two services. This conclusions is reinforced by the parallel result obtained from the Downriver project. Finally, OJT is not found to have a significant effect on reemployment, suggesting that its use in the Buffalo project as a job placement tool may have been unnecessary.

NOTES

1. Two recent books supply useful information on the design and operation of JTPA programs. Levitan and Gallo (1988) is a comprehensive qualitative assessment of all of JTPA's components, while Cook (1987) contains case studies of nine operating projects funded by Title III of JTPA.

2. Title III also requires that states match federal grants dollar for dollar. However, the burden imposed on state treasuries is lightened by allowing (1) state matches to be in-kind as well as in cash and (2) part or all of the match to be forgiven for states with unemployment rates above the national average.

3. The flip side of this argument is that early intervention is inefficient if services are provided to workers who would have otherwise found jobs on their own, or if workers do not yet face sufficient economic pressure to seek alternative employment or to enter a retraining program.

4. The description of the ETP program is primarily based on Employment Training Panel (1984, 1985, 1986, 1987) and Arthur Young (1985).

5. ETP provides funds only for the reimbursement of actual training costs incurred by employers or training agencies. Funds may not be spent to subsidize the wages paid to trainees or to pay income maintenance allowances. Similarly, ETP does not support remedial education.

6. During its early years, the Panel used "master contracts" with state agencies and business and training organizations as an administrative tool to carry out the dual objectives of providing training and fostering economic development. For example, under a master contract with the Los Angeles Community College District, the Panel authorized a variety of training projects to meet the needs of Los Angeles employers. More recently, however, the Panel has determined that master contracts are ineffective and their use has been abandoned.

7. In January 1987, a third state—North Carolina—passed legislation to cut employers' UI payroll taxes and simultaneously assess a new payroll tax earmarked to finance a worker training trust fund. A commission has been appointed to study how best to utilize the trust fund.

8. Planning information for the Delaware program was provided by a randomized experiment carried out between late January and early July 1983 by the Delaware Department of Labor. The design and results of the experiment are discussed in chapter 3.

9. On the other hand, Stevens (1986:29) makes the point that employers are quickly learning that the states are serious about sharing in training expenses without being intrusive in the trainee-selection process. He goes on to suggest that states must move quickly to assess their priorities in preparing to formalize criteria to be used in distinguishing between employers applying for limited training funds.

10. Although the employer makes the actual contribution, Hamermesh (1977:10–15) provides an interesting discussion of the possibility that the source of funds used to pay the UI tax may be consumers if the tax can be shifted forward, or employees if the tax is shifted backward.

11. Temporary public sector employment is currently viewed as a method for allowing the most disadvantaged to acquire the work experience that will lead to eventual private sector MEED placement.

12. Stevens (1986:25) makes the same point in connection with Massachusetts' Bay State Skills Corporation. This is a training program which attempts to foster partnerships between state postsecondary schools and employers with skill-training requirements. Targeted populations are displaced workers, minorities, and the economically disadvantaged.

13. The only source of funding for the 2000 Fund was voluntary contributions by business firms in exchange for a credit on the state corporate income tax. Not surprisingly, the tax credit incentive proved insufficient to encourage substantial business contributions to the program.

3
Job Search Assistance Programs

As noted at the beginning of chapter 2, the basic presumption of retraining programs is that displaced workers lack the vocational skills— either transferable or firm-specific—that would qualify them to compete for vacant jobs in their local labor markets. The presumption underlying job search assistance (JSA) programs, in contrast, is that displaced workers already possess the necessary vocational skills to compete. Rather, their reemployment is delayed for one of three reasons: (1) lack of knowledge about how to go about searching for a job, (2) lack of motivation to engage in search, or (3) lack of interest in the jobs that are available. Lack of knowledge is a problem for many displaced workers because, as long-term employees in their previous jobs, their job search skills were largely unused and have become rusty. Lack of motivation to search may occur because of the work disincentive associated with the UI system. Finally, as emphasized in chapter 1, the unattractive prospect for some displaced workers of having to accept sharply reduced wages and benefits reduces the odds of an early acceptance of a job offer.

The work disincentive factor is the topic of a large body of literature. As originally pointed out by Feldstein (1974), the provision of UI income support reduces the cost of not working, which tends to increase the length of recipients' job search. More recently, Kingston, Burgess, and St. Louis (1986) and St. Louis, Burgess, and Kingston (1986) provide evidence that many UI recipients substantially overreport their actual job search effort in order to comply with the UI "work test" (i.e., the requirement that UI claimants be actively seeking employment). This evidence suggests that for some workers, UI benefits may actually be subsidizing leisure and nonmarket pursuits rather than job search. Burgess and Kingston (1987) discuss in detail the adverse incentives

53

built into the UI system, along with the problems of program complexity and ineffective claimant monitoring, and offer a number of suggestions for reforming the existing system.

In connection with JTPA Title III programs, chapter 2 also pointed out that program developers are under considerable pressure to reduce per participant costs while attempting to maintain high placement rates. This pressure, as well as questions about the effectiveness of retraining and the desire of many program participants to get back to work as quickly as possible, has led most Title III projects to place substantially more emphasis on JSA than vocational training. The first section of this chapter outlines the component services commonly found in JSA programs including those funded by Title III. This discussion provides the background information needed for understanding the details of particular JSA programs.

The remainder of the chapter is divided into three substantive sections, which are distinguished by the type of JSA program considered. The first of these sections outlines five experimental programs intended to increase job search skills. Available for four of these programs is evaluation evidence drawn from a comparison of randomly selected treatment and control groups. The other two sections investigate two alternative approaches to JSA, both of which have the objective of increasing the motivation to engage in active job search. The reemployment bonus experiments carried out in Illinois and New Jersey are examined first. Then considered are demonstration projects in Charleston, South Carolina and Washington state which were intended to test the effectiveness of more closely monitoring the search activity of UI claimants. The chapter concludes with a summary section.

Components of JSA Programs

In describing the individual services typically provided in JSA programs, JSA will be defined broadly so that the services discussed range from initial outreach to terminal job placement activities. Such a broadly defined JSA program is included, for example, as the first of three treatments in the New Jersey Unemployment Insurance Reemployment

Demonstration Project initiated in October 1985.[1] It should be noted, however, that the term JSA is often defined more narrowly to include only individual job search training services and job development and job matching (items 4 and 6 discussed below). The services are discussed in roughly the sequential order in which they are generally offered.

1. *Outreach.* The first problem is to make known to displaced workers the services offered by a JSA program. With respect to workers affected by a plant closing or mass layoff, the surest means of making contact is to offer assistance at the plant site before layoffs begin. Chapter 4 goes into more detail on site-specific services, including a discussion of advance notification requirements and early warning systems. For other unemployed workers, outreach depends more on media campaigns, word of mouth, and referrals from local Job Service offices of state Employment Service (ES) agencies.

2. *Orientation.* Orientation plays the key role of informing prospective participants about the services offered by the program, what these services can and cannot be expected to deliver, and what is expected of the participants themselves. The objective is to help unemployed workers arrive at a sensible decision regarding program participation. In particular, unemployed workers anticipating recall and those who can reasonably be expected to find satisfactory jobs without assistance should be discouraged from continuing further. Helpful in this regard is the clear acknowledgement by project staff members that there is no guarantee that jobs available to program graduates will offer prelayoff levels of pay and benefits. Potential participants should especially be cautioned that not everyone benefits from relatively costly and time-consuming retraining programs.

3. *Assessment and testing.* In many JSA programs, the next service provided is an assessment intended to determine whether a participant already possesses locally marketable skills or whether retraining is necessary for reemployment. Formal testing is often used to determine the participant's vocational interests and his or her aptitude for undertaking particular retraining programs. In some cases, testing may reveal that remedial education is a prerequisite for retraining. For example, Kulik, Smith, and Stromsdorfer (1984:46) point out in their evaluation of the Downriver demonstration project that despite fairly high levels

of educational attainment (close to 60 percent of program-eligible workers had completed high school), some 20 percent of participants scored below sixth grade levels on standardized reading and math tests administered by the program. The report also notes that the two-week assessment and job search training sequence used in the Downriver project served the purpose, among other objectives, of screening out those participants who lacked the motivation to actively pursue reemployment.

4. *Job search workshops.* Based on the assessment results, participants are typically channeled into either a classroom training or OJT program or enrolled in a job search workshop. Job search workshops generally last about 20 hours spread over four or five days. Workshop content usually consists of two primary elements. First, specific job search skills are taught, including resume preparation, techniques for locating job leads, and effective application and interviewing practices. Second, motivational activities and exercises are provided to raise the low self-esteem that many displaced workers suffer after being laid off.

Following the job search workshop, most programs make available a "resource center" which participants can use as a base of operation for their self-directed job search. Resource centers are typically outfitted with a telephone bank, telephone and business directories, newspaper help-wanted ads, and listings of job openings from the local Job Service office. An important objective of resource centers is to create an atmosphere of mutual encouragement and support by encouraging job searchers to operate out of a common location.

A second logical follow-up to the job search workshop is the formation of a job club in which club members meet on a regular basis to telephone employers for job leads. Job clubs allow for the supervised application of recently acquired job search skills and offer the opportunity for developing a group support system during the search period. Drawing on the experience of the Dislocated Worker Demonstration project, Corson, Maynard, and Wichita (1984:132–34) describe a successful implementation of the job club concept in the Lehigh Valley program. A key feature of this program was a fixed membership per club of about 15 participants that was unchanged until all club members obtained jobs. The reduction in the number of club members as placements occurred had a positive rather than a negative effect on remaining members and the project staff since job club moderators took pride in watching the club "close-out." The authors also caution, nevertheless, that because of the highly personal interaction likely to be generated in job clubs, they may not be appropriate for all clients or in all areas.

5. *Counseling.* Most JSA programs provide some form of follow-up counseling at regular intervals. Corson, Maynard, and Wichita (1984:134) note that counseling at the six sites of the Dislocated Worker Demonstration project ranged on a continuum from informal, occasional counseling largely consisting of job interview advice to sophisticated case-management systems which assigned clients to particular counselors who were given full responsibility for the client's progress through the program. Whatever form the counseling takes, its primary goal is to insure that program participants are making satisfactory progress in their job search. Particular services a counselor can provide include (1) serving as a "sounding board" for participants, (2) providing job information and arranging for support services, (3) urging clients to make use of resource center facilities, (4) providing coordination with job development activities, and (5) encouraging participants to persevere in their search.

6. *Job development and job matching.* In addition to training the individual unemployed worker to locate his or her own job, some JSA programs also offer the service—called job development—of utilizing the informal contacts of staff members to turn up job openings that are not advertised. That is, the function of a job developer is to uncover job vacancies that would be unlikely to come to the attention of displaced workers searching on their own. The OTA report (1986:249) notes that job development is successful when job developers earn the confidence of local employers by carefully screening workers for job openings. With program staff doing the screening, employers need interview only a few well-qualified applicants. Kulik, Smith, and Stromsdorfer (1984:44) provide the following description of the dynamic nature of the job development process:

> Perhaps the most significant aspect of the DCC [Downriver Community Conference] program's job development strategy was its continued intensity. Program staff kept an ever-

expanding file of employers and contacted each one every
month to inquire whether their hiring needs had changed or
whether the program could assist them in any way. Even if
an employer had already hired participants, staff made the
contact to ask if there were additional openings. Such efforts
in some instances resulted in placement of several workers
within one firm. Such continuous monitoring of employers'
situations also enhanced the likelihood that Downriver staff
would be in the right place at the right time, should an
employer develop a vacancy.

Job matching typically involves storing participant information (e.g.,
test scores, vocational interests, and background) organized by occupational code. When a job order is produced by a job developer, the participant file is accessed to identify appropriate referrals. Files of prospective candidates are then reviewed, often in consultation with the
counselors responsible for particular individuals. Once a tentative selection is made, the participants are notified, and, if they are interested,
an interview is arranged.

Programs to Enhance Job Search Skills

The OTA report (1986:248) remarks that training in job search skills
is valuable because many displaced workers do not know how or where
to look for employment. Often, the report points out, displaced workers
have had only one job in their lives, and they got it by just showing
up at the plant gate. Five state-sponsored experiments intended to test
the effectiveness of alternative JSA services in enhancing the job search
skills of displaced workers are examined in this section.

The Delaware Dislocated Worker Pilot Program

Between late January and early July 1983, the Delaware Department
of Labor conducted a randomized experiment to assess the impact of
alternative services in increasing the earnings of displaced workers and
in reducing their need for UI benefits. The four basic services were
job search workshops, individual counseling, job development, and

retraining. Information from the program was to be used in planning Delaware's JTPA displaced worker program. As noted in chapter 2, a statewide program in Delaware was begun in 1984.

Although the pilot program achieved the quite high placement rate of 80 percent for program participants, the econometric analysis reported by Bloom (1987) indicates that there is no significant difference between the treatment and control groups in either UI benefit payments or short-run earnings. An extremely small sample size—only 65 persons in the treatment group and 110 in the control group—leads to large standard errors, however, making it unlikely that precise program impacts would be detected.

Of perhaps more interest than his empirical results are Bloom's recommendations based on qualitative evidence regarding the three JSA services (job search workshops, counseling, and job development) included in the Delaware pilot program. Using information gained from site visits and discussions with program staff members, he draws the following conclusions.

1. Staff members frequently complained that some participants lacked motivation to engage in job search. Program changes suggested by Bloom thus include (1) more detailed interviews by program staff and (2) more motivational hurdles at the outset of the program (e.g., further individual assessment and required participation in more preliminary orientation activities). The more comprehensive initial screening of participants would hopefully have the effect of restricting program services to those who really need them and are likely to benefit.

2. The four to five half-day job search workshops were perceived by both participants and staff as quite valuable. Given the amount of material covered (i.e., assessment of individual career goals, putting together a resume, interview preparation, uses of media and other job information, and self-directed job finding approaches), Bloom recommends that the workshops be continued and extended in length.

3. The counseling and job development roles were performed by separate groups of persons on loan from area high schools and community colleges. The provision of both of these services would be strengthened if (1) counselors and job developers devoted more of their time to the program and (2) the counseling and job development ser-

vices were more closely linked. Corson, Maynard, and Wichita (1984:134) reinforce this conclusion, pointing out that the absence of coordination means that job developers work with little detailed knowledge of the employment strengths and weaknesses of individual participants. At the same time, counselors and participants operate without detailed information on area employers and specific job openings.

The Wisconsin ERP Pilot Project

In contrast to the Delaware program, the Wisconsin ERP Pilot Project concentrated on just one JSA service—job search workshops.[2] As described by Jaggers et al. (1984), the objective of the project was to determine the effect on UI benefit expenditures of mandatory attendance at a one-day, six-hour workshop. The project involved a sample of 4,276 indefinitely separated UI claimants who were randomly assigned to treatment and control groups (the treatment group consisted of 1,999 individuals). Workshops were conducted at six sites between March and August 1983. Unfortunately, the design of the pilot project does not allow for an assessment of the impact of differences in workshop content and methodologies between sites.

The principal result of the ERP project is that the treatment group is found to have received on average 0.62 fewer weeks of UI benefits than the control group. Spread over the entire sample of claimants, the 0.62-week difference amounts to a gross saving of $164,837 in UI benefit expenditures. Of this figure, $11,438 is due to the denial of one week of benefits to treatment group claimants who failed to attend a workshop. The implication is that the remaining saving of $153,399 can be attributed to workshop attendance. Total project costs were approximately $50,000.

As was the case for the Delaware program, the qualitative reaction to the ERP workshops was highly favorable. Nearly all of the claimants who attended a workshop reported that they benefited from the experience. Similarly, district Job Service directors at the project sites and workshop staff members were unanimous in supporting the continuation of this JSA service. Jaggers et al. (1984:5) conclude that in a period of high unemployment and ES understaffing due to federal cutbacks, job search workshops represent an efficient use of UI resources in terms of both the effective utilization of ES employment assistance expertise and the preservation of the state's UI trust fund.

JSA Services in the New Jersey UI Reemployment Demonstration Project

Possibly the most ambitious experiment designed to measure the effectiveness of JSA services (as well as other types of reemployment assistance) is the New Jersey UI Reemployment Demonstration Project. The U.S. Department of Labor initiated the project, and it is operated as a joint venture by the USDOL and the New Jersey Department of Labor. Implementation began in July 1986.

An overview of the demonstration. The New Jersey demonstration has two primary objectives. The first is to assess the feasibility of an "early intervention" strategy. At issue are the questions of whether and how it is possible to use the UI system to identify early in the claim period unemployed workers who are likely to exhaust benefits but are unlikely to return to their old or similar jobs. "Early" is defined operationally as the fifth week of claiming UI benefits. The second objective is to empirically measure the effectiveness of three alternative packages of reemployment services in accelerating the return to work. JSA, which is designated Treatment 1, is the first of the three. Treatments 2 and 3 are, respectively, JSA plus an offer of either training or relocation assistance and JSA plus an offer of a reemployment bonus.

Concerning the first objective, the basic problem is to distinguish displaced workers from those who are unemployed for other (cyclical, frictional, or seasonal) reasons so that appropriate services can be provided early in the spell of unemployment. The Unemployment Insurance Service report (1986:6) describing the New Jersey demonstration points out that the clearest way to make this distinction is by looking at the length of completed unemployment spells. The longer the spell, the more likely it is that the unemployed worker is truly displaced. But, as the report notes, *ex post* information on length of spells is not very helpful in making *ex ante* decisions on which claimants should be targeted for assistance.

The approach taken in the demonstration project is to apply five "screens" during the fourth week of claiming benefits. The cumulative effect of these screens is to define displaced workers as unemployed workers on permanent layoff who are 25 years of age and older and who had at least three years of tenure with their last employer prior to being laid off. Over 7,000 claimants who passed through these screens were randomly selected for the experiment and offered demonstration services.

Turning to the second objective of the demonstration, a full range of JSA services is included as part of Treatment 1. These services include orientation, testing, a job search workshop, a resource center, an assessment/counseling interview, and job referral. Following the assessment/counseling interview, participants are expected to have a specific job goal, an "employability plan" directed at achieving that goal, and a working knowledge of how to effectively use a resource center. Periodic follow-up contacts are scheduled following the assessment interview.

It should be emphasized that these JSA services are above and beyond those currently provided to unemployed New Jersey residents. That is, unemployed workers assigned to both the treatment group and the control group would be eligible for JTPA Title III services, they would be referred to the ES for placement assistance, and they would participate in the UI work search process. The demonstration services differ from those currently offered in that claimants in the demonstration have a considerably higher chance of receiving the (JSA or retraining/relocation) services, and the demonstration services are generally provided earlier in the unemployment spell. In each of 10 demonstration sites, current and demonstration services are provided by four-person teams consisting of three ES staff members and a JTPA staff member from the local Service Delivery Area.

Preliminary results. An interim report by Corson and Kerachsky (1987) discusses preliminary results for the first six months of program operation following its implementation in July 1986. Regarding the demonstration's first objective, the report notes that it is not yet possible to determine whether the five screens satisfactorily identify claimants who, in the absence of additional employment services, would experience difficulty in becoming reemployed. Nevertheless, the screens do appear to restrict the demonstration-eligible population to persons whose attributes are usually associated with displaced workers and reemployment difficulty. For example, sizable fractions of the demonstration population are male, displaced from jobs in manufacturing, and black or Hispanic. Cases in which the screening procedure tended to break down include individuals from growing industries like services, and claimants who eventually returned to their former employer and presumably did not require reemployment services.

Preliminary evidence on the net impact of the three treatments on weeks and amount of UI benefits is presented in table 3.1. (Later reports are to include estimates of treatment effects on employment and earnings.) Estimates shown are the treatment group mean minus the control group mean. The JSA-only treatment is seen to decrease length of UI benefits by slightly over half a week and amount of benefits by nearly $88. The estimated effect on weeks of UI benefits is quite comparable to the estimate of 0.62 of a week obtained for job search workshops only in the Wisconsin ERP project.

Table 3.1
Estimated Treatment Effects for the New Jersey
UI Reemployment Demonstration

Outcome measure	JSA only	JSA plus training/ relocation	JSA plus reemployment bonus
Weeks of UI paid	−0.54	−0.49	−0.64
Dollars of UI paid	−$87.55	−$69.42	−$171.72

SOURCE: Corson and Kerachsky (1987, Table 4, p. 21).

Looking across treatments, the results in the table are generally consistent with *a priori* expectations. In particular, the reemployment bonus is expected to have the largest impact because of the substantial reemployment incentive created by the bonus. (This result will be discussed in more detail later in the chapter.) Corson and Kerachsky (1987:21) note that the estimated differences between the bonus treatment and the JSA-only treatment are statistically significant. It is also expected that the training/relocation treatment will have the smallest immediate effect on UI receipt, since individuals undergoing training continue to receive UI benefits. The benefit of training in terms of economizing on UI costs should occur in the longer run as retrained individuals enjoy more stable employment. The small differences seen in table 3.1 between the JSA-only and the JSA plus training/relocation treatments are not statistically significant. Also contributing to the small estimated differences is the low participation rate of 14 to 16 percent of those offered the training/relocation option.[3]

The Texas Worker Adjustment Demonstration (WAD) Projects

It is useful to compare the preliminary results from the ongoing New Jersey demonstration to the findings of the completed Texas WAD projects. Carried out during 1983–85 by the Texas Department of Community Affairs, WAD involved some 2,250 Title III JTPA program participants in two projects in El Paso and one in Houston. It is important to note that the Texas demonstration projects represent the first attempt to apply an experimental design methodology to an evaluation of continuing Title III programs.

As described in the report by Bloom and Kulik (1986), the experimental design of the WAD projects included random assignment of Title III program participants to either of two treatment groups or to a control group. The first treatment group received JSA services only (Tier I). Core JSA services provided at all three sites included orientation, job search workshops, assessment, and job development and placement. Members of the second treatment group received JSA followed, if necessary, by more expensive classroom or OJT retraining (the Tier I/II sequence). The control group was supplied all non-Title III services available in Texas.

In addition to the Tier I and Tier I/II distinction, there were also important differences between sites. In Houston, participants tended to be prime-age white males, while Hispanic females were heavily represented in the two El Paso sites. Overall, nearly 40 percent of WAD participants were women. Only for the Houston site could the differential effect of the additional services in the Tier I/II sequence be distinguished from the Tier I JSA-only services. The available comparison for the El Paso sites is limited to the Tier I/II sequence and the control group.

The WAD demonstration yielded three main results. As summarized in table 3.2, the first is that program participants experienced short-run positive impacts on earnings and weeks worked as well as a decrease in dollars received in UI benefits. (The ambiguous findings for female participants in Houston appear to be due to the small sample size.) Second, these impact estimates tended to be larger and more pronounced for women than for men. In particular, female participants in El Paso experienced a program-induced gain in annual earnings of $1,070. The gain in annual earnings for men in Houston and El Paso ranged from $750 to $770. Since the mostly male Houston participants earned more than twice as much as the mostly female El Paso participants prior to WAD enrollment, the gender difference in estimated earnings gains is even more striking when expressed in percentage terms.

Table 3.2
Estimated Program Effects for the Texas WAD Projects

	Men		Women	
Outcome measure	**Houston**	**El Paso**	**Houston**	**El Paso**
Annual earnings for the year after random assignment	$750	$770	0	$1,070
Weeks worked for post-assignment quarters 3 and 4	2.1	0.7	1.7	3.1
Total UI benefits for 30 weeks after random assignment	–$210	–$170	$200	–$130

SOURCE: Bloom and Kulik (1986, Exhibit 7.2, p. 171).

The third result (not shown in table 3.2) involved the differential effect of Tier I versus Tier I/II services. For males in Houston, the effect of retraining services (which were almost exclusively classroom training) was to *decrease* both earnings and employment relative to the effect of JSA-only. For example, the earnings gain for the year after random assignment was $860 for Tier I-only participants as compared to only $680 for Tier I/II participants. Bloom and Kulik (1986:173) take considerable pains to qualify this result. Most important, they note that the technical-vocational classroom training provided in Houston was of limited interest to participants, who were predominantly highly-paid former petrochemical workers. This mismatch between partici-pant interests and available retraining options resulted in low participation in the training component of the Tier I/II sequence, and it undoubtedly contributed to the negative incremental effect estimated for classroom training. For future Title III programs, Bloom and Kulik (1986:181) conclude that (1) JSA should be the core service provided and (2) skill training should be used sparingly for well-specified needs and only where adequate local training resources are present.

The Washington Claimant Placement Project

The final JSA program summarized in this section is the Claimant Placement Project first authorized in 1985 as a two-year pilot project by the Washington state legislature. One important feature of this pro-gram is its funding. As described in chapter 2, funding is provided through an earmarked tax of 0.02 percent on employer payrolls, with an offsetting reduction in UI tax rates of 0.02 percent for most employers. Also worth noting is the project's explicit goal of protecting the solvency of the state's UI trust fund by reducing the average length of claimants' unemployment spells. The method by which this objective is to be ac-complished is individualized JSA services provided early in the period of UI eligibility.

To provide some assurance that sufficient job openings will be available to match up with unemployed workers, the project selected 20 Job Service offices located in local labor markets identified as hav-ing the greatest potential for claimants to return to work quickly. From each of these 20 offices, project staff members work with claimants from the onset of their UI claims through approximately the tenth week of unemployment. A full mix of JSA services is offered including skill assessment and testing, job search workshops, job matching, and job development.

Two JSA services of particular interest are the comprehensive employability plan worked out for each claimant and the First Source Hire Program. A recent report of the Washington State ES Department (1987) details the elements of an employability plan as including (1) a listing of the claimant's skills and experience, (2) notice of any factors hindering job search (e.g., lack of child care), (3) identification of suitable occupations and a reasonable expected wage rate, (4) a plan consisting of specific action steps leading to employment, (5) recognition of any additional social services necessary to overcome barriers to employment, and (6) a signed commitment by a project staff member and the claimant to follow through with the plan.

The First Source Hire Program allows a claimant to try out a job for 30 days while continuing to draw UI benefits. The idea behind the program is to provide the employer a chance to assess a claimant's job performance before putting him or her on the payroll. The ES department report notes that the JSA service making the most difference for project claimants is the employability plan. Unfortunately, there is currently no quantitative evaluation evidence publicly available.

In the spring of 1987, the Washington state legislature took action to permanently fund the Claimant Placement Project—but with an interesting change in emphasis. Whereas services provided by the pilot project were available to almost any UI claimant on permanent layoff, the 1987 legislation gives priority to older workers and the long-term unemployed. The former group is defined as UI claimants 50 years of age and older. The ES department is delegated the responsibility of identifying the latter group subject to the guideline that the long-term unemployed are to include those demographic groups of UI claimants with the highest percentages of persons who have either drawn at least 15 weeks of UI benefits or exhausted their UI eligibility. The enabling legislation singles out these two groups to receive special JSA services because they are thought to be less likely than the general population of claimants to find new employment at wages comparable to their prelayoff earnings.

The Reemployment Bonus Concept

While the previous section focused on programs designed to enhance job search skills, the introduction to this chapter pointed out that the reemployment of displaced workers may also be delayed by a lack of motivation to engage in search or by the natural reluctance to accept a new job offering considerably lower wages and benefits. This section describes two experiments designed to test the impact of a reemployment bonus in stimulating the intensity of job search and the willingness to accept offered jobs. Since the reemployment bonus is a new concept, the results of these experiments are being closely studied by policymakers interested in innovative approaches for reducing UI outlays and the length of insured unemployment spells.

The Illinois UI Experiment

Between mid-1984 and mid-1985, the Illinois ES department conducted a controlled experiment involving two types of reemployment bonuses. In the Claimant Bonus Experiment, a random sample of new UI claimants was told that they would receive a cash bonus of $500 upon reemployment.[4] The intent of this experiment was to encourage more intensive job search and faster reemployment. In the Employer Bonus Experiment, another random sample of new UI claimants was told that, once a hiring commitment was made, the employer of each newly hired claimant would be eligible for a $500 cash bonus. Here the intent was to test the effect of a marginal wage-bill subsidy (or training subsidy) in reducing the duration of insured unemployment.

Bonuses in both experiments were paid only if hiring (of 30 hours or more per week) occurred within 11 weeks of the initial claim and if the job lasted at least four months. The 11-week period was chosen because it was one to two weeks less than the median duration of insured unemployment in the state. The four-month job duration requirement was imposed to reduce the possibility that a claimant would accept a temporary or seasonal job simply to obtain the bonus. Roughly 4,000 UI claimants between the ages of 20 and 55 were randomly assigned to each of the two treatment groups and to the control group.

As reported by Woodbury and Spiegelman (1987), the main results of the Illinois UI experiments include the following:

1. Important differences were found in claimants' willingness to participate in the two experiments. About 84 percent of those eligible for the Claimant Experiment agreed to participate, as opposed to just 65 percent of those offered the chance to participate in the Employer Experiment. A similar difference in actual use of the programs was also detected. Only 3 percent of Employer Experiment enrollees were responsible for a bonus payment to their employers, whereas 14 percent of Claimant Experiment enrollees earned a bonus for themselves.

2. Comparing the entire Employer Experiment treatment group to the entire control group, there is no significant difference in either UI benefits paid or weeks of insured unemployment, where both outcome variables are measured over the full benefit year. This result is not surprising, given the limited participation in the program and the very small percentage of employers who actually received bonuses.

When white women are analyzed separately, however, enrollment in the Employer Experiment is found to unambiguously reduce both UI benefit payments and weeks of insured unemployment. White female enrollees received $164 less in UI benefits and experienced one full week less of insured unemployment (over the full benefit year) than did white women randomly assigned to the control group. White women were the only race-sex group that experienced a statistically significant effect in this experiment.

3. In contrast to the generally insignificant Employer Experiment results, the Claimant Experiment is found on average to have reduced UI benefits by $158 and duration of insured unemployment by 1.15 weeks, where both outcome variables are measured over the benefit year. These estimates are obtained for all workers assigned to the Claimant Experiment, whether or not they agreed to participate, and whether or not they actually received bonus payments. When the average $158 reduction in UI benefits is multiplied by the over 4,000 Claimant Experiment assignees, Illinois saved roughly $660,000 relative to what its UI benefit expenditures would have been in the absence of the program. Bonus payments to eligible claimants amounted to $285,000, so

that unemployment benefits were reduced by a striking $2.32 for every $1 in bonuses paid out to claimants by the state.

Woodbury and Spiegelman (1987:527) also point out that if the Claimant Experiment were implemented in a full-scale program, the take-up rate would undoubtedly be higher than it was in the experiment. The experiment's take-up rate of 0.545 is calculated by dividing the proportion of claimants receiving a bonus (0.136) by the proportion qualifying for a bonus (0.250). A higher take-up rate would have the effect of reducing the benefit-cost ratio for the program. But even in the unlikely event of a 100 percent take-up rate, the benefit-cost ratio would fall to only 1.26, which implies that the Claimant Experiment would reduce UI benefit expenditures by considerably more than the bonus costs incurred.

4. A possible explanation of the effect of the Claimant Experiment in reducing length of unemployment is that program participants may have accepted a less favorable match between worker and job (thereby sacrificing earnings) in order to qualify for the $500 bonus. A comparison of postprogram earnings across the treatment and control groups indicates, however, that this is not the case. More consistent with the evidence is the hypothesis that the faster reemployment resulted from more intense job search effort by Claimant Experiment participants.

The Reemployment Bonus Treatment in the New Jersey Demonstration Project

The encouraging response of UI claimants to the Illinois Claimant Experiment program suggests that it might be useful to explore further the potential of the reemployment bonus concept. A desirable extension of the Illinois experiment would be to make the size of the bonus conditional on the length of job search. Treatment 3 of the New Jersey UI Reemployment Demonstration Project is a reemployment bonus the size of which hinges on a claimant's remaining UI "entitlement." Remaining entitlement is defined as the lump-sum payment representing the stream of benefit payments to be received over the remaining weeks of UI eligibility.

The New Jersey reemployment bonus treatment works as follows. Treatment group members pass through the sequence of JSA services (orientation, testing, and a job search workshop) to the assessment/counseling interview which occurs in the seventh week of the benefit period. In the course of their interviews, claimants selected for this treatment are informed of the specifics of the bonus program. If they decide to participate, they can collect the maximum bonus by locating and accepting a job during the next two weeks. The maximum bonus is specified to be one-half of the claimant's total entitlement. After the two-week period has passed, the size of the bonus will decrease by 10 percent per week, reaching zero at the end of the eleventh week after the assessment/counseling interview (the eighteenth week of the entitlement period).

A concern of program designers was that the bonus be structured so that it would not encourage claimants to take minimum wage or very short-term jobs. The Illinois experiment dealt with this problem, as noted, by requiring full-time employment lasting at least four months. Treatment 3 participants in New Jersey are required to obtain full-time employment lasting four weeks in order to qualify for a bonus. Moreover, two additional provisions are built into the program to encourage participants to seek "appropriate" employment. First, counselors are to inform participants in the assessment/counseling interview of the potential long-term earnings loss that would result from accepting a low-wage job just to get the bonus. Second, the bonus payment is divided into two lump-sums, with receipt of the second lump-sum contingent on continued employment for 12 weeks.

Corson and Kerachsky (1987:18) report that the bonus receipt rate is about 20 percent.[5] About one-quarter of those who earned the bonus received the maximum of $1,600, and most others received over 60 percent of the maximum (the mean expected bonus is about $1,300). Given the limited experience to date, the authors indicate that the average job for which the bonus is claimed starts about four weeks after the assessment/counseling interview.

Returning to the estimates shown for the New Jersey demonstration in table 3.1, the incremental effects of the reemployment bonus are a reduction in the average duration of insured unemployment by 0.10 of a week and a decrease in UI benefit expenditures of $84.17. These estimates are substantially smaller than the corresponding estimates of

1.15 weeks and $158 obtained for the Illinois Claimant Bonus Experiment. Since the average bonus payment is more than twice that paid out in Illinois, the cost effectiveness of the Illinois claimant bonus program does not appear to carry over to the New Jersey experiment. The New Jersey program pays out $260 (= .20 x $1,300) to save about $84 in UI payments. Nevertheless, as argued by Corson and Kerachsky (1987:21), the truncation of the observation period means that the estimates presented in the table are likely to underestimate the ultimate effect of the reemployment bonus (as well as that of the other two treatments).

As a final comment on the reemployment bonus concept, Woodbury and Spiegelman (1987) make the point that the bonus paid to workers can be viewed in the context of either a job search model or an income-leisure model of labor supply. In the labor supply context, the bonus raises the opportunity cost of leisure consumed during the time period immediately following the initial claim, thus creating an incentive to substitute income for leisure. From this perspective, a reemployment bonus represents a wage-subsidy to workers which should help to overcome their reluctance to move to jobs paying lower wages but offering superior career opportunities.

Programs to Monitor Job Search

In addition to paying bonuses to stimulate job search intensity, the incentive to engage in active job search may also be increased by raising the probability that claimants who fail to meet the UI work test will be detected and their names removed from UI benefit rolls. This section discusses two demonstration projects intended to test the effectiveness of alternative approaches to monitoring and directing the search activity of UI claimants.

The Charleston Claimant Placement and Work Test Demonstration

Carried out during the period from February through December 1983, this demonstration project involved over 5,000 UI claimants in the

Charleston, South Carolina area who were randomly assigned to three treatment groups and a control group. All three treatment groups received a "strengthened work test" implemented by sending a call-in notice to claimants at the time their first UI check was issued requiring them to register at a local Job Service office within one week or face a possible loss of benefits. This delayed registration requirement represented a change from standard procedures in several ways. First, it exempted from registration ineligible and job-attached claimants, thereby allowing the ES to focus its attention on those who might benefit most from its services. Second, it provided a definite date by which registration was to occur. Third, the registration requirement was explicitly monitored by a computerized matching of UI call-ins and ES registration files. Finally, when a match was not found, the claimant was sent a notice to report for a fact-finding interview, and no benefits were paid until he or she had reported. Treatment Group 3 received only the strengthened work test, as well as the same services provided all other ES applicants.

Treatment Group 2 differed from Group 3 in that, in addition to the strengthened work test, its members received more intensive job placement services than those customarily provided. In particular, Group 2 claimants were offered a placement interview during which they were placed in the job-matching system. After the placement interview, claimants considered job-ready could also expect to receive either a job referral or a job development attempt. Those claimants who were still unemployed nine weeks later were sent a second call-in notice requiring a return visit to the ES. Enhanced placement services were also provided during this second visit.

Treatment Group 1 claimants were offered the same services as provided Group 2, with the addition of an opportunity to participate in a three-hour job search workshop. The workshops were offered to claimants who had been collecting UI benefits for four weeks. The special call-ins involved in Groups 1 and 2 services also increased the ability of the ES to provide information to enforce the UI work test. Group 4, the control group, was told about the services available at ES offices but not required to report.

The main results of the Charleston demonstration are described in Corson, Long, and Nicholson (1985) and summarized in table 3.3. Relative to the experience of the control group, the strengthened work test applied to claimants in Group 3 reduced length of UI benefits by slightly over half a week and the amount of benefits by about $53. The JSA activities provided to claimants in Groups 1 and 2 further reduced per claimant UI expenditures, particularly the addition of the job search workshop for Group 1 claimants.

Table 3.3
Estimated Treatment Effects and Costs
for the Charleston Demonstration Project

Outcome measure	Treatment Group[a]		
	1	2	3
Reduction in mean UI benefits			
Weeks collected	0.76	0.61	0.55
Dollars collected	$73.14	$58.71	$52.93
Net additional administrative			
cost per claimant	$17.58	$13.17	$4.72

SOURCE: Corson, Long, and Nicholson (1985: Table V.1, p. 104).

a. Treatment Group 3 received only the strengthened work test. Group 2 received enhanced job placement services plus the strengthened work test. Group 1 was offered a job search workshop in addition to enhanced job placement services and the strengthened work test.

Taking account of administrative costs, the final row of the table indicates that for each dollar spent on administering the strengthened work test, UI expenditures were reduced by an amazing $11.21. The addition of enhanced job placement services for Group 2 claimants increased administrative costs by more than its small impact in reducing UI benefits. On the other hand, the job search workshop added for Group 1 claimants decreased UI payments by more than the associated increase in administrative costs. Treatment 1 is therefore cost effective relative to Treatment 2.

Corson, Long, and Nicholson (1985:106–108) interpret their results as suggesting that there is no strong evidence that the treatments affected the reemployment success of claimants, either by encouraging more active job search or by helping claimants to find jobs more rapidly than they would have otherwise. Rather, it appears that the reporting requirements, coupled with the cessation of UI payments for failure to report, were the most important reasons why the treatments led to a reduction in UI expenditures. Claimants tended to leave the UI rolls either because they were formally denied benefits or they simply stopped claiming benefits. From an overall policy perspective, the Charleston demonstration indicates that the manner in which the UI work test is monitored does matter.

The Washington Alternative Work Search Project

The second demonstration project examined in this section is similar in design and orientation to the Charleston demonstration, but it places less emphasis on work test monitoring and more emphasis on alternatives for structuring UI claimants' work search effort. Located in Tacoma, Washington, the demonstration began on July 1, 1986 and was to continue for five quarters through the end of September 1987. Results are as yet unavailable.

Like the Charleston project, claimants in the Tacoma demonstration are randomly distributed across three treatment groups and a control group. Treatment 1 represents a radical departure from current policy. Claimants are instructed that they are expected to conduct an active search for work, but there is no monitoring of their search by the local Job Service office. The only requirement for continued UI benefit eligibility is that claimants call in whenever there is a change in their eligibility status (e.g., positive earnings or employment, ceasing to look for employment, or unavailability for work). The basic question addressed by this treatment is whether current monitoring and reporting requirements affect the motivation to seek work and the duration of unemployment.

Treatment 2—the control group—subjects claimants to current work search policy. That is, following ES registration compliance with the UI work test is implemented by requiring all claimants, excluding those on temporary layoffs, to make three employer contacts per week. Claimants' self-reported search activity is monitored by local Job Service officials on a weekly basis. The only reemployment service provided claimants is an Eligibility Review Interview (ERI) conducted during the thirteenth week of unemployment (which is the average duration of unemployment for the state). The intent of the ERI is to advise claimants of continued eligibility requirements and to discuss work search techniques. Underlying this treatment is the premise that intervention in the search process is a low priority use of scarce resources in comparison to the timely payment of benefits. In meeting the specific needs of displaced workers, it is perhaps worth noting that the Secretary of Labor's Task Force (1986:33) recommends that the ES be restructured to more effectively and efficiently deliver labor market adjustment services.

Treatment 3 represents a more activist approach to assisting the return to work. The main change from current policy is to tailor search requirements to the needs of individual claimants and to local labor market conditions. In particular, the required number of contacts per week is made more flexible depending on the claimant's occupation and particular reemployment problems. The work search requirement expressed in terms of contacts per week becomes more intensive, however, as length of unemployment increases. The ERI is also moved up in the claim period to as early as the fourth week for claimants in high-demand occupations.

Treatment 4 is similar to Treatment 3 except that instead of the earlier ERI, its main form of intervention is an intensive two-day job search workshop scheduled for the fourth week of unemployment. Intervention in the fourth week is based on the presumption that if unemployment lasts more than a few weeks, the claimant is probably in need of JSA services. Workshop services include skill assessment, interviewing and marketing techniques, telephone canvassing, and job development. The workshop is followed by three weeks of telephoning employers using the facilities of resource centers.

Summary

Following a description of individual job search assistance services, this chapter focused on three types of JSA programs. A common objective of all three types is to speed up reemployment in order to reduce UI benefit expenditures. The different categories of programs are distinguished by the problem perceived as causing the reemployment process to be delayed. The most noteworthy feature of the evaluation evidence presented in the chapter is that the three types of JSA programs have all been subjected to evaluation using controlled experiments with random assignment.

The first type of JSA program is directed at the problem that displaced workers may possess the vocational training but lack the job search skills necessary to locate new employment expeditiously. Programs intended to enhance job search skills typically include a mix of services including orientation, assessment and testing, a job search workshop, counseling, and job development and job matching. Such JSA programs are widely available under Title III of the Job Training Partnership Act. Described in detail in this chapter are the JSA experiments carried out in Delaware, Wisconsin, New Jersey, Texas, and Washington state. The evidence produced from the Wisconsin, New Jersey, and Texas experiments indicates substantial program effects measured in terms of reducing weeks of unemployment and level of UI benefits paid out. For the other two programs, the size of the sample available for the Delaware pilot project is probably insufficient for drawing reliable statistical inferences, and quantitative evidence is not available for the Washington project. It should be noted, however, that both the Delaware and Washington experiments have led to permanent state-funded programs.

A second type of JSA program is directed at the problem that reemployment is delayed because UI claimants lack the motivation to actively engage in job search. An innovative approach to stimulating the intensity of job search is the reemployment bonus. Examined in this chapter are two experimental programs designed to test the effectiveness of the reemployment bonus concept. Results from the completed experiment in Illinois and preliminary results from the New Jersey experiment indicate that a reemployment bonus paid to workers (although not to employers) can reduce the length of unemployment and associated UI outlays. A striking finding from the Illinois experiment is that UI benefits were reduced by $2.32 for every $1 in bonuses paid out to claimants by the state.

The third type of JSA program is based on the hypothesis that alternative procedures for monitoring and directing the search activityof UI claimants would increase, relative to current practices, the intensity of job search. A test of this hypothesis has been carried out in Charleston, South Carolina and is currently being conducted in Tacoma, Washington. The Charleston demonstration project suggests that strengthening and regularizing the way initial ES registration is handled can make a substantial difference in UI benefit expenditures. Rather than speeding up reemployment, however, the saving in UI expenditures appears to have been mostly due to an increase in the denial of benefits because of claimants' failure to satisfy the UI work test and to persons failing to continue to apply for benefits in the early weeks of their claims.

A common theme in the experimental results reported for all three types of programs is the significant impact of JSA in reducing UI benefit expenditures. Reinforcing these favorable results are JSA impact estimates on short-term earnings and reemployment opportunities obtained from the federally-funded Downriver and Buffalo demonstration projects. In the case of the Buffalo project, for instance, Corson, Long, and Maynard (1985:112) report that program participants who received JSA services earned $134 more in the first six months after the program ended than did members of the control group. Since JSA services are relatively inexpensive to provide, their favorable impact on UI benefit expenditures means that JSA programs are quite likely to be cost effective.

NOTES

1. The second and third treatments are, respectively, JSA plus an offer of either training or relocation assistance and JSA plus an offer of a reemployment bonus.

2. ERP stands for "Eligibility Review Process," a term used in federal UI regulations to refer to the process of promoting active job search by UI claimants. Because the job search workshops were viewed as assisting claimants in their job search, UI funds could be used to underwrite the cost of employing ES staff to conduct the workshops.

3. Corson and Kerachsky (1987:15) note, consistent with other evidence, that fewer than 1 percent of those offered relocation assistance used it.

4. The $500 figure represented a balance between the budget constraint of the experiment and an arbitrary judgment about how small a bonus could still be expected to elicit a response. For the average UI claimant, $500 was approximately 5 percent of annual wage and salary earnings, and represented about four weeks of UI payments.

5. An additional 10 percent of Treatment 3 claimants stopped collecting UI but failed to collect a bonus. Claimants falling into this 10 percent are likely to have been ineligible for a bonus because they either returned to their former employer or they obtained part-time or seasonal work.

4
Advance Notice and On-Site
Delivery of Services

Chapters 2 and 3 discussed, respectively, state initiatives in vocational training and job search assistance (JSA) programs. Relatively little attention in those chapters was devoted to the questions of where the programs should be physically located and when the services should be offered. This chapter examines these two questions in the context of on-site delivery of reemployment services. On-site programs are generally of short duration and are timed to either precede or closely follow the announcement of a layoff or plant closure.

Concerning the location in which reemployment services are provided, the Office of Technology Assessment report (1986:234) makes the following argument favoring on-site programs:

> Some of the best-run displaced worker projects are those centered in plants that are closing or undergoing large layoffs, and are operated by people who work at the plant on both the labor and management sides. Plant-centered projects have several advantages in their favor: the people who run them have a personal stake in the outcome, know many of the individual workers involved, and are acquainted with the local business community where the hidden job market (openings that are never publicly announced) is found.

Although it is not explicit in this quotation, the author of this section of the OTA report almost certainly had in mind the operation of on-site programs sponsored by the Canadian Industrial Adjustment Service (IAS). The IAS program serves as a model for the state rapid-response team initiatives discussed later in the chapter.

Before leaving the location question, it should be noted that, despite this chapter's focus on site-specific programs, the great majority of displaced worker programs in the U.S. are neither located at the plant nor temporary. Programs operated beyond plant gates by continuing outside organizations are necessary because a large layoff or plant closing typically has a ripple effect in the community causing other firms, especially suppliers to the closed plant and local retail and service outlets, to terminate employees.

Regarding the timing of adjustment assistance, most analysts suggest that policy intervention is most effective if it is in place before layoffs begin (see, for example, Fedrau 1984:86). Although not all displaced workers will opt for immediate program participation, making reemployment services available early offers several advantages. First, displaced workers can be identified and offered program services before they disperse following layoffs. Second, program staff members are given an opportunity to counsel workers on the need to adjust to the new labor market realities they face and to assist them in planning a systematic job search strategy. In addition to minimizing the loss of earnings and benefits associated with layoffs, the early formulation of a job search strategy helps to avoid the bitterness and breakdown in self-respect that often accompanies the unexpected loss of a long-held job and the resulting period of inactivity. Finally, early intervention provides workers who choose to enroll in a retraining program the full 26 weeks of income maintenance furnished by UI.[1] It is also worth emphasizing that JTPA Title III funds can only be used to assist workers who have already received a termination notice. Thus state-funded programs fill an important gap in assisting displaced workers before they are laid off.

A precondition for effective early intervention is that policymakers are aware of the imminence of a mass layoff or plant closure. This chapter begins with a discussion of advance notice legislation and early warning systems. After describing state advance notice laws and the new federal Worker Adjustment and Retraining Notification Act, the first section examines the limited number of empirical studies of the effectiveness of prenotification.

The next section provides an overview of the rapid-response programs in place in many states to deliver reemployment services on-site to displaced workers. Included is a discussion of the highly regarded Canadian IAS program. A final section summarizes the chapter.

Advance Notice and Early Warnings Systems

Early warning of a planned plant closure or mass layoff can be obtained in either of two ways.[2] First, employers can be asked (voluntary advance notice) or mandated (required advance notice) to inform policymakers in advance of the date of a planned layoff or plant closing. Alternatively, a state may develop its own early warning system for identifying troubled firms. This section begins with an examination of the advance notice issue. Then state early warning systems are briefly discussed.

Advance Notification

Current and proposed legislation. During the past 20 years the states of Maine, Wisconsin, and Hawaii have enacted mandatory advance notice laws. In addition, at least two other states have legislation encouraging employers to voluntarily give advance notice of layoffs and plant closings,[3] and a number of other states are considering advance notice legislation. The first state plant closing law was adopted in Maine in 1971. As originally passed, the Maine law covered all firms with more than 100 employees and required that employees be given one month's notice of an intended closing. The penalty levied against employers for failure to give notice was one week's pay for every year worked (up to a maximum of one month's pay) for every employee with at least one year of seniority. During the years that followed, the law was amended several times. From 1974 to 1982 the employee notification provision was dropped, and employers were only required to notify the director of the state's Bureau of Labor. The law currently requires that an employer relocating outside the state must give 60 days' advance notice to employees and to the director of the Bureau of Labor. Also included in the law is a provision requiring one week's severance pay per year of service for displaced workers with more than three years of seniority.[4]

In Wisconsin, plant closing legislation was passed in 1976 and amended in 1984. The law currently requires 60 days' notice of a plant closure affecting at least 10 employees by any firm with 100 or more employees in the state. Notification must be received by affected workers, their collective bargaining representative, local community officials, and the state's Department of Industry, Labor, and Human Relations. Employers who fail to comply with the notification requirement are subject to a fine of $50 per employee laid off.

The most recent piece of state plant closing legislation was signed into law by the Governor of Hawaii on July 7, 1987. This law requires employers with 50 or more workers to give 45 days' advance notice of a planned layoff. Notice must be provided in writing to all affected employees and to the state's director of Labor and Industrial Relations. Penalties for noncompliance are twofold: (1) affected employees have the right to sue the employer for damages and (2) the employer is subject to a fine equal in value to three months' wages and benefits for each laid-off employee.

Turning to the national level, Hamermesh (1987) reports that an advance notice bill—the Labor-Management Notification and Consultation Act of 1985—came within five votes of passage in the House of Representatives. This bill would have mandated at least 90 days' prior notification of a permanent layoff or plant closing involving more than 50 employees. Dropped on the House floor from the final version of the bill was a provision requiring employers to consult "in good faith" with representatives of employees on alternatives to a scheduled closing or layoff.

More recently, the highly controversial advance notice provision originally attached to the Omnibus Trade and Competitiveness Act of 1988 required that firms employing 100 or more workers must give 60 days' notice of a plant closing. In the case of a layoff, the bill required the 60 days' notice if the layoff involves 50 or more workers representing at least one-third of the workforce at a place of employment. Firms violating the advance notification requirement would be obligated to provide back pay to employees for each day of notice not given (up to a maximum of 60 days of wages) and to pay fines of up to $500 per day to their local governments. It is interesting to note that the final version of the bill approved by a House-Senate conference committee omitted a House provision requiring employers, after giving notification, to consult with unions on proposals to forestall closures or large layoffs.

In addition to exempting small firms from the notification requirement, the 1988 act specified a number of other situations in which an employer scheduling a shutdown would not be required to give advance notice. Specifically, exemptions from the notification period would be permitted in the event of unforeseeable business circumstances or in cases in which a "faltering" employer was actively seeking additional capital or new orders to avoid or postpone shutting down. Other exemptions included plant closings caused by the sale of the business, relocations within a community if workers were offered new positions, and closing of temporary facilities or completions of particular projects.

In May 1988, President Reagan vetoed the entire trade bill, principally because of his opposition to the mandatory advance notice provision. The House voted immediately to override the veto, but the 61 to 37 vote in the Senate fell short of the two-thirds majority needed to override. Subsequently, however, prenotification became a hot issue during the 1988 presidential campaign; and political pressure for the passage of some form of advance notice legislation was overwhelming. In July 1988, Congress passed the conference committee version of the bill under the title, the Worker Adjustment and Retraining Notification (WARN) Act. The act finally became law in early August when President Reagan decided against vetoing the trade bill a second time.

Empirical studies. Despite the recent intense policy interest in plant closing regulation, relatively little has been done in attempting to empirically measure the relationship between advance notice and the subsequent unemployment and earnings experience of displaced workers. There are four major studies available at this time.

In the earliest of these studies, Folbre, Leighton, and Roderick (1984) examine the plant closing legislation adopted in Maine. Although the Maine law currently makes advance notice mandatory, during the 1974–82 time period examined by the authors the law required employers only to notify the director of the Bureau of Labor of a closing. Since the director treated as confidential the notifications he received, whether or not affected workers received advance notice was at the option of the employer. The resulting *voluntary* notification of workers permits a comparison to be made of the effects of notified and unnotified plant closings on local unemployment rates.

The methodology applied by Folbre, Leighton, and Roderick involves regressing local unemployment rates on three sets of explanatory variables: (1) the number of workers laid off in major plant closings expressed as a percentage of the local labor force (current and seven lagged values of this variable are included); (2) a dummy variable representing advance notice of at least one month prior to a plant closing interacted with the layoff rates; and (3) control variables, including the state unemployment rate and a set of dummy variables measuring area-specific factors (other than plant closings), that might affect unemployment rates. The advance notice-layoff rate interaction terms permit the impact of advance notification to be measured conditional on the level of the layoff rate. The empirical analysis uses a pooled time-series/cross-section data set which includes monthly data for the 1974–82 period measured across 15 labor market areas in Maine.

The regression results reported by Folbre, Leighton, and Roderick indicate that advance notice significantly diminishes the unemployment impact of layoffs in the month of the plant closing. Specifically, advance notice is estimated to reduce the effect of layoffs from 0.8 to 0.3 unemployed workers in the local labor market area for every worker laid off in that month. The effect of advance notice on total unemployment measured over a six-month period can also be obtained by summing the estimated coefficients on the current and lagged values of the layoff variables and the advance notice-layoff rate interaction variables. Carrying out this calculation, the authors find that advance notice lowers total unemployment from five to four worker-months for every worker laid off. (It should be emphasized that these six-month estimates include the ripple effect of a layoff so that what is measured is aggregate worker-months of unemployment per worker laid off and not average months of unemployment experienced by a laid-off worker.)

In interpreting their results, an important point made by Folbre, Leighton, and Roderick is that the effect of advance notice on unemployment rates need not occur through the more rapid reemployment of displaced workers. It is also possible that a decrease in unemployment may occur via migration from the local labor market or complete withdrawal from the labor force. The authors report results from an auxiliary analysis showing that advance notice does decrease the size of the local labor force, but they are unable to distinguish between labor force withdrawal and outmigration (and possible reemployment elsewhere).

The provocative, if tentative, findings of Folbre, Leighton, and Roderick receive support from a study of individual-specific data by Addison and Portugal (1987b). The 1984 DWS data set discussed in chapter 1 includes a question that asked displaced workers whether or not they received advance notice or otherwise expected to be laid off. Addison and Portugal make use of this key piece of information in examining the effect of advance notice on the length of unemployment spells of workers laid off because of a plant closing or relocation. Serving as control variables in their regression analysis are a varietyof individual worker attributes including years of schooling, sex, race, predisplacement wage and years of tenure, and receipt of UI benefits.

The main results of the Addison-Portugal study are the following:

1. Advance notification of an impending layoff is strongly and inversely related to weeks of unemployment. Advance notice is found to reduce the average length of unemployment spells by about four weeks or nearly 28 percent.

2. The relationship between advance notice and unemployment hinges on the receipt of UI benefits, with benefits sharply reducing the effect of advance notice. Hence, the negative relationship between advance notice and unemployment duration holds mainly for those who did not receive benefits. This result can be best understood by noting that a worker who is eligible for UI by virtue of being unemployed has not been able to exploit the information conveyed in advance notification by locating a new job prior to the announced date of plant closure. In other words, the notified displaced worker receiving UI benefits is in much the same position as one who did not receive notification

3. The impact of advance notice on unemployment is also found to be significantly affected by a dummy variable measuring, for those who received advance notice of a layoff, the effect of quitting prior to the plant closing date. Inclusion of the "early leaver" variable reduces the estimated effect of advance notification by about 45 percent. This result reinforces the conclusion that the driving force behind the negative

advance notice-unemployment relationship is the impact of prenotification in stimulating early job leaving.

Addison and Portugal point out three qualifications that should be kept in mind in interpreting their results. First, DWS data provide no information on the length of advance notification. To the extent that the period of advance notice is short, the effect of a policy-induced lengthening of the notification period will be understated. A recent USGAO study (1987b:34–35) points out that the usual period of notice is indeed quite short. Based on a survey of business firms that experienced a plant closure or made permanent layoffs, the USGAO reports that about one-third of the employers surveyed provided no notice at all and less than 20 percent provided notice of more than 30 days. The median length of notice was seven days.

A second qualification is that the DWS does not contain information on JSA services often offered in conjunction with advance notice. The same USGAO report (1987b:46–47) notes that about one-third of the firms surveyed offered job search assistance, and about 20 percent offered career and personal counseling.[5] If, as expected, JSA services speed up the reemployment process, the omission of these services has the impact of upwardly biasing the estimated effect of advance notice on unemployment duration.

The final qualification of the Addison-Portugal results is that, as noted, the advance notice measure available in the DWS includes respondents expecting to be laid off in addition to those who received advance notice of a layoff. Thus, the "treatment group" is contaminated by the inclusion of an unknown number of respondents who did not actually receive notice but who instead accurately predicted the closing of their plants. Swaim and Podgursky (1988:11) argue reasonably that workers receiving formal advance notice are likely to be more aggressive in their predisplacement search than those who merely expected to be laid off. If this is the case, measurement error in the notification variable will tend to bias downward the estimated impact of advance notice.

The third major study is the examination by Swaim and Podgursky (1988) of the impact of advance notice on duration of joblessness using a pooled sample of displaced workers from both the 1984 DWS and the 1986 DWS.[6] The conventional treatment of advance notice as a dummy variable implicitly assumes that notification only has an effect on postlayoff search. The main innovation of the Swaim-Podgursky study is the specification of an empirical model that explicitly allows job search to commence prior to layoff for workers receiving advance notice. The modeling of predisplacement search as qualitatively different from postdisplacement search makes sense for two reasons: (1) the financial pressure to engage in search is lower before the layoff date than after, and (2) continued employment between the dates of notification and layoff absorbs time that potentially could be invested in search activities.

The empirical results obtained by Swaim and Podgursky indicate that advance notice significantly accelerates reemployment for males in blue-collar and white-collar (including service) jobs and for white-collar females. This effect is primarily due to the fact that notified workers are more likely to find a new job before layoff and thus report zero weeks without work. By way of contrast, it is interesting to note that in an earlier study, the same authors report a significant effect of advance notice only for white-collar women (see Podgursky and Swaim 1987c). Also worth noting is the Swaim-Podgursky finding that the rate of reemployment falls sharply as jobless spells increase in length. This negative "duration dependence" implies that although many displaced workers become reemployed with little or no joblessness, a substantial minority have severe adjustment problems and suffer prolonged spells of unemployment. Demographic groups at high risk of long jobless spells are found to include older workers, blacks, workers with little schooling, and single men. Labor market characteristics associated with lengthy spells include long job tenure, industry unionization rate, and area unemployment rate.

Swaim and Podgursky next use their results to simulate the effect on jobless duration of varying lengths of advance notice. For blue-collar males (by far the largest of the four groups examined), eight weeks of advance notice compared to no notice reduces the expected length of a jobless spell from 51.0 weeks to 48.1 weeks. Using market wage levels to measure the foregone earnings associated with joblessness, benefits for blue-collar males rise from $539 for four weeks of advance notice to $1,572 for twelve weeks of notice.

The final empirical study, by Ehrenberg and Jakubson (1988), takes advantage of detailed industry and state information available for 1984 DWS respondents to create a merged data set containing an extensive list of industry- and area-specific variables. These variables include area unemployment rates, percent unionization by area, estimated three-digit industry wage premiums, and industry employment growth rates. Among the major findings of the study are the following:

1. There is little support for the hypothesis that workers who received advance notice paid for it by accepting lower predisplacement wages. Nor were the authors successful in explaining the incidence of prenotification using data on individual and industry characteristics and on employment growth and unemployment rates. In analyses such as the four studies reviewed here, it appears that advance notice can legitimately be treated as exogenously determined.

2. Advance notice did significantly increase the probability that a displaced worker would *not* experience any unemployment. Once unemployment is experienced, however, receipt of notification does not appear to affect the ultimate duration of joblessness. This result reinforces the Addison-Portugal and Swaim-Podgursky conclusion that advance notice primarily operates by stimulating early job leaving, thus moderating increases in local unemployment rates.

3. There is no evidence that receipt of advance notice has any significant impact on postdisplacement weekly earnings measured as of the January 1984 survey date for workers displaced during the 1979–83 period. Podgursky and Swaim (1987b) report the same result for workers displaced from full-time jobs.

4. For DWS respondents who received advance notice, the authors were unable to find evidence indicating that variables that might serve as proxies for productivity (such as job tenure, schooling, or previous earnings) were systematically associated with the probability that a worker might quit prior to the date of his or her displacement. Thus, there is essentially no support based on DWS data for the hypothesis that prenotification would lead the firm's most productive workers to quit their jobs prior to the plant closure.

Benefits and costs of advance notice. Subject to the qualifications noted, particularly with respect to DWS data, the available empirical studies provide limited evidence supporting what is probably the most important benefit of advance notification legislation. This is the point that by speeding up the reemployment process, advance notice reduces the adjustment costs of displacement discussed in chapter 1.[7] The resulting cost reduction represents both a private benefit to workers and a social benefit from the viewpoint of society.

The empirical evidence does not provide sufficient detail to offer a behavioral explanation of how the reemployment process is expedited. But a closely related benefit is that advance notice provides lead time prior to a layoff or plant closing for policymakers to plan and put into place a program of worker adjustment assistance. In this connection, the recent GAO report (1987b:32–33) notes that in Canada, comprehensive advance notice laws require between 56 and 112 days of notice, and that officials of the Canadian IAS program argue that it takes the bulk of the required time to effectively prepare for a plant closing. Evidence summarized in the National Academy of Sciences study indicates further that workers are more likely to enroll for reemployment assistance if the programs have the cooperation of management and are available prior to layoff (see Cyert and Mowery 1987:155–56). One other policy-related benefit is that advance notice provides time for government officials to search out new owners for facilities slated for closure and to assist employee groups in organizing a buyout attempt.

Given the probable benefits of advance notice legislation, the key policy issue is whether these benefits outweigh the costs imposed on employers when the government mandates a period of notice that differs from the notice agreed to voluntarily by workers and employers as part of the compensation package. One factor representing a private cost to employers is that by reducing the firm's flexibility in making layoffs, advance notification increases the fixed costs of employment. Greater fixed costs affect the demand for labor by causing employers to hold back on hiring commitments until they can be reasonably sure that workers hired can be kept on the payroll long enough to recoup the fixed costs. Workers just worth hiring are now priced out of the market.

A series of recent editorials in *The Wall Street Journal* make the argument that the much higher rate of employment growth in the U.S. than in Western Europe since 1970 is due, at least in part, to a difference in the cost of hiring and laying off workers. For example, Drouin (1986) writes that in Common Market countries:

> [R]igid dismissals legislation has transformed labor costs into fixed costs. The ensuing inflexibility increases overall business costs and risks. Again most countries, notably France, are introducing measures to facilitate hiring and firing. Most countries are allowing increased use of fixed-term contracts. Italy is relaxing recruitment regulations. But, generally, layoffs continue to require discretionary decisions by government and lengthy negotiations. The cost of dismissal remains steep.

Lazear (1987) also concludes from his reading of the European experience that legislation that protects a worker's right to a job will benefit some individuals at the expense of others. Incumbent job holders are likely to benefit from job security policies, while the young and the unemployed will be hurt. In his view, the record indicates that the number of jobs lost far outweighs those retained.

A second cost-side consideration mentioned in connection with the Ehrenberg-Jakubson study is a possible negative effect of advance notice on worker productivity. One reason is that a termination notice may reduce employee morale and encourage shirking during the notification period. Also contributing to lower worker productivity is the possible effect of advance notice in encouraging early quits, thereby risking the loss of crucial employees and potentially crippling reductions in the size of the workforce.

Finally, employers frequently make the third cost-side argument that advance notice invites contentious efforts by unions and other employee groups to alter the decision to close a plant. White (1988) provides an interesting description of the backlash that has occurred when parent companies try to close plants after having earlier accepted tax concessions and subsidized loans offered by states and local communities to preserve jobs. Actions taken by local government officials to keep plants in their communities from closing include breach-of-contract suits, product boycotts, and court injunctions preventing the transfer of capital equipment to other plants.

The balance of opinion among labor economists and policymakers appears to favor requiring employers to provide advance notice of plant closings or permanent layoffs. On the benefit side, the empirical articles surveyed in this section indicate that advance notice does facilitate the adjustment of workers into new jobs prior to their date of displacement. On the cost side, in contrast, the fragmentary evidence currently available fails to suggest that advance notice requirements impose substantial private costs on employers. Regarding the argument of higher fixed costs, Abraham and Houseman (1988) conclude from their analysis of time-series manufacturing data for Germany and the U.S. that there is no strong evidence that the quite restrictive and controversial dismissal legislation passed in Germany in the early 1970s affected subsequent adjustment practices.[8]

Concerning workers' productivity and morale, the Ehrenberg-Jakubson findings confirm the results of an early case study by Weber and Taylor (1963) of 32 plant shutdowns which shows that there was no perceptible decrease in productivity following the announcement of a plant closing. Weber and Taylor suggest, in fact, that the spread of rumors concerning an impending plant closure may be more destructive to morale and productivity than a formal announcement of the shutdown. More recently, the National Academy of Sciences report (see Cyert and Mowery 1987:157) concludes that

> [T]he productivity and quality *improvements* that occur [during the advance notice period] appear to reflect the reaction of employees to the evidence that management is concerned about their welfare, the operation of counseling and job search programs that begin prior to layoff, the resolution of anxieties and uncertainties, and the desire of workers concerned about reemployment to demonstrate to new employers that the quality of the work force in the closed plant was high. [Emphasis added.]

Fedrau (1984:84) and the Secretary of Labor's Task Force (1986:22–23) reach similar conclusions.

It should also be mentioned that there is a conceptual counterargument to the cost-side point that advance notice has the effect of increasing fixed costs of employment. The counterargument is that while advance notice may increase the private costs borne by employers, failure to provide advance notice imposes substantial costs (or "externalities") on workers and communities not shared by the firms closing plants or laying off workers. Advance notification requirements may thus be viewed as a mechanism for ensuring that employers bear (or "internalize") a portion of the costs they impose upon others. In other words, such requirements help to cushion workers from the full adverse consequences of free market decisions, making it politically possible to avoid the sort of heavy government intervention often practiced abroad.

Given the widespread support for some form of plant closing regulation, it is interesting to speculate on the reasons underlying the intense opposition of many business groups to the modest advance notice requirement enacted in the 1988 WARN bill. Addison (1988) suggests that this opposition has less to do with the specifics of the notification requirement than with the fear that this piece of legislation represents an opening wedge for the introduction of far more coercive and costly forms of government intervention. His argument is that the federal budget deficit and taxpayer resistance to tax increases severely constrain federal policymakers from directly providing such widely discussed employment benefits as universal health insurance, parental leave, and child care. Thus the natural response of those who seek to extend worker entitlements is to mandate employers to foot the bill for such services.

State Early Warning Systems

A number of states have also proceeded independently of employers in developing their own early warning systems to identify firms experiencing financial difficulty and to indicate needed changes in state economic policies. To date, no assessments of these systems have been carried out, and little is known about the importance the states themselves attach to internally generated early warning signals. This section contains a brief overview of the early warning programs of a few selected states and some associated empirical evidence.

Balderston (1986) describes the early warning systems in place in Connecticut, Rhode Island, and Arizona. In Connecticut, the Department of Economic Development has attempted to piece together a historical record of every company that closed in the state and the reasons for each failure. A predictive model based on these data is then used to provide forecasts of which existing firms and plants may be at risk of shutting down, and field staff members are assigned to work with these employers to increase their chances of survival. Balderston notes that the business failure data have also been found useful in contributing information on needed adjustments in state policies.

It was pointed out in chapter 2 that the thrust of economic development programs in some states has shifted from attracting new firms to retaining existing firms. In the geographically small state of Rhode Island, the Department of Economic Development surveys each employer in the state on an annual basis as part of its business retention program. The purpose of the interviews is to gauge the attitude of the business community toward the state's economic climate and to determine how state government can assist in lowering operating costs and expanding markets. In Arizona, similarly, a Governor's Task Force recently surveyed existing firms as well as employers who left the state or chose not to locate in Arizona in an attempt to assess the effectiveness of current state economic policies.

Beyond these three states, still other states have recently taken action to establish early warning systems. In Massachusetts, the Mature Industries Act passed in 1984 provides for an early warning system intended ". . . to identify industries and businesses likely to experience large losses in employment or plant closures. . . ." In carrying out this objective, the Act directs a designated state agency—the Massachusetts Industrial Service Program—to collect and analyze information on product markets experiencing declining growth rates and on industries subject to competition from Third-World countries. This agency is also given the responsibility to monitor changes in patterns of company ownership, employment, and layoffs; of UI contributions; and of state corporate tax payments. Since 1984, Nelson (1986; 1987) reports that Missouri and New Jersey have both established commissions charged with developing early warning signals to identify industries beginning to decline and firms in danger of closing.

Recent research by Howland (1988) helps in our understanding of what factors are important determinants of plant closures and relocations. Using Dun and Bradstreet's Dun Market Identifiers file, she merged into a single data set time-series observations for 1973, 1975, 1979, and 1982 for each of approximately 54,000 establishments in three narrowly defined manufacturing industries (metal working machinery, electronic components, and motor vehicles). Among her major findings are the following:

1. The most important predictor of whether a plant will close is the plant's status as a branch, subsidiary, headquarters, or independent (single-plant operation). Branches and subsidiaries are found to close at much higher rates than headquarters and independents. An implication of this finding is that economic development strategies should emphasize the promotion of start-ups and expansions of locally owned firms. In addition, Howland suggests that local takeovers of marginally profitable branches and subsidiaries provide largely untapped opportunities to keep these plants operating.

2. Local economic conditions including relative wage levels, utility costs, taxes, and rate of unionization do not strongly influence the probability of a plant closure. This finding implies that local public policies, including lowering tax rates, curbing utility costs, and discouraging unionization, will not be effective in retaining jobs. Such policies may even be counterproductive if they reduce the level of local income and tax revenues.

In addition to Dun and Bradstreet data, a potentially quite important source of information on plant closures is the Permanent Mass Layoff and Plant Closing (PMLPC) program of the Bureau of Labor Statistics. This federal-state program, initially established in 1984 for eight states, uses data from each state's UI data base to identify and track workers affected by major plant closings and layoffs. In 1987, the survey covered 29 states and included information on 1,687 establishments that reported 2,020 major layoffs affecting 406,887 workers. It is expected that the program will become nationwide during 1988.

The way the PMLPC program works is that state UI data bases are used to identify establishments with at least 50 initial claims filed against them during a three-week period. Within each state, these establishments are then contacted by telephone by the state's employment security agency to determine the total number of persons separated, the reasons for these separations, whether the separations are permanent or temporary, and whether or not the establishment is remaining open. The resulting PMLPC data set merges information collected from two different sources: (1) state UI data bases which supply information on the personal attributes of individual claimants such as sex, age, race, ethnicity, and residence, and (2) telephone contacts with employers which provide information on establishment characteristics including location and industry. Until regular UI benefits are exhausted, the continuing impact of a permanent layoff or plant closing can be tracked by matching affected initial claimants with continued claims filed under regular state UI programs.

On-Site Delivery of Services

On the presumption that policymakers are informed of an imminent plant closing, the next question is the most effective way to deliver reemployment services to workers scheduled to be displaced from their jobs. The OTA report (1986:238) points out that the value of advance notification is greatly diminished if high-quality reemployment services are not offered during the lead time notification provides. An important aspect of policy intervention during the notification period is that affected workers are given a structure on which they can pattern their job search activities. The idea is that displaced workers who are engaged in active job search are less likely to lapse into a destructive loss of self-confidence that may otherwise accompany a permanent job loss.

Before proceeding further, it is important to make a distinction between two types of on-site programs. The first involves the on-site delivery of formal vocational training programs to workers who have not received notice of termination but who cannot expect to retain their present jobs if their skills are not upgraded. An example of this type of on-site initiative is the computer numerical control machining program provided by California's ETP program (see Arthur Young 1985:16-17).[9] Serving employees of three large aerospace firms in southern California, this program brings a mobile training facility (i.e., a training trailer) to the site of each participating company. In contrast, the second type of on-site program is intended to provide predominantly

JSA services to workers who have received notice of a permanent separation from their jobs. It is the second type of program which will be discussed here.

Recent discussions of on-site JSA programs have featured prominently the Canadian IAS program. For example, one of the major recommendations of the Secretary of Labor's Task Force (1986) is to create a worker adjustment service in each state modeled along the lines of the IAS. The examination of the IAS program is followed by a description of existing state rapid-response team programs.

The Canadian IAS Program

Established in 1963, the IAS is a federally-funded agency intended to serve as a catalyst in bringing together local labor and management officials to locate job oppportunities for workers displaced by economic and technological change. The IAS is very small in terms of number of employees and size of budget. Its staff consists of 60 experienced professionals, with only three persons located in its headquarters offices in Ottawa and the rest assigned to regional field offices. Its annual budget in recent years has been between $6 and $8 million (in Canadian dollars).

As described in the Secretary of Labor's Task Force report (1986:21), the IAS program operates on five premises.
   1. Reemployment services should be offered in advance of, rather than after, a plant closing or mass layoff.
   2. Advance warning is essential to allow time for planning and implementing appropriate reemployment services.
   3. Worker adjustment to displacement is best accomplished by the joint action of the parties directly involved.
   4. The role of government is to encourage and support, not to supplant, the efforts of management and labor.
   5. Program participation should be voluntary.

After learning that a plant closing is imminent, the IAS acts immediately to meet with labor and management representatives at the highest possible level and to offer its assistance in finding new jobs for laid-off workers. Early warning of a layoff is quite likely because six of the ten Canadian provinces have plant closing laws that require 8 to 16 weeks' advance notice of layoffs affecting 50 or more workers. In addition, a national advance notice law applies to government-owned enterprises such as airlines and railroads.

If the IAS's offer of assistance is accepted, which is nearly always the case, the agency negotiates a brief formal agreement which provides for the establishment of an ad hoc labor-management adjustment committee consisting of an equal number of labor and management representatives. Labor representatives include prospective job losers wherever possible. The purpose of the agreement is to obtain from both the employer and the union (if a union is present) a commitment of time and financial resources to the adjustment process. The IAS also provides a chairman, whom the adjustment committee may select from a roster of experienced people. In addition, it pays half of the committee's costs, with the company usually picking up the other half. Committees typically finish their work and disband in about one year. The IAS arranges from 400 to 600 labor-management agreements per year.

The basic strategy of the IAS is to place unemployed workers in jobs that are never publicly announced, but instead are filled by word-of-mouth. From this strategy follow several of the important features of the program. One of these is an emphasis on prompt placement rather than retraining, relocation, or counseling. Adjustment committees not only undertake to uncover job openings, but they also attempt to make it easier for prospective employers to consider client workers by assisting in the screening process. Workers who cannot be placed because of a need for retraining are referred to Canada's extensive adult vocational training system.

A second feature of the IAS's strategy is recognition that it is people with extensive experience in the industry and community—that is, the labor and management representatives on an adjustment committee— who are in the best position to use their informal contacts to engage in job development. Thus the IAS advisor to an adjustment committee keeps a low profile, and the committees themselves are flexible enough to look at the individual needs of each worker. Worth emphasizing is the basic philosophy of the IAS that displaced workers are to be assisted individually by persons who know them personally.

The OTA (1986:23–24, 55, and 167) and the Secretary of Labor's Task Force (1986: Appendix A) comment favorably on the operation of the IAS. Noted in particular are the program's modest cost (about $171 per year for every worker served), reasonably good placement rates (about two-thirds of workers affected by plant closings are placed within a year), absence of bureaucratic red tape, and contribution to improved labor-management relations. The Task Force report also mentions that a survey of displaced workers served during the 1982–83 fiscal year indicated that IAS assistance reduced the length of unemployment spells by an average of two weeks, with the resulting saving in unemployment insurance benefits.

One other indication of the interest of U.S. policymakers in the IAS program is the implementation in January 1987 of a demonstration program—the Canadian-American Plant Closing Demonstration Project—to help determine whether the Canadian model can be transferred to the U.S. Jointly sponsored by the USDOL and the National Governors' Association, six states including Iowa, Michigan, New Jersey, New York, Ohio, and Vermont, were selected to participate in the project. In each state, at least two sites have been selected to test the impact of adjustment committees in assisting the reemployment of displaced workers in a variety of different settings. Salzman (1987) reports that the project has already caused several states to rethink the administration and operation of their displaced worker programs.

State Rapid-Response Teams

Of existing labor market initiatives in this country, the one that probably comes closest to the IAS is the state rapid-response team concept. Balderston (1986:39) reports that over 20 states have established rapid-response teams to coordinate the delivery of services on-site to displaced workers. A representative example of this coordination is the New Jersey Labor Response Team program established in December 1984. The program is operated by the state's Department of Labor.

Following notification of a plant closure or mass layoff, representatives of relevant state agencies arrange for a meeting with management officials to discuss the economic status of the company. If a plant closure or layoff is determined to be unavoidable, the range of available state reemployment services is reviewed, and the meeting concludes with an agreement on the plan of action to be taken and the date for a response team to make an on-site presentation to affected workers.

A response team consists of staff members of New Jersey's ES and UI divisions, the Division of Employment and Training, and the local Service Delivery Area of the Title III JTPA program. A variety of topics are discussed by teams in the on-site sessions. These include an expedited process for registering for UI benefits, the requirements for continued eligibility for UI coverage, an ES-sponsored job search workshop, and the retraining opportunities available in Title III programs. The job search workshop, in particular, is sold as a service especially designed for people who have not been obliged to look for a job in recent years because they have been continuously employed.[10] Two themes emphasized in the sessions are that (1) a displaced worker should not feel that he or she is alone, since the phenomenon of permanent mass layoffs and plant closings is a common one in New Jersey and across the nation; and (2) it is important to take prompt advantage of the adjustment services offered.

The available evidence indicates that employer awareness of the New Jersey program is growing and that more firms involved in curtailing operations or shutting down plants are contacting the state's Department of Labor and providing time and space on-site for team presentations. For the period between July 1, 1986 and March 31, 1987, the program estimates that 11,461 potentially displaced workers were offered adjustment assistance services.

Other state rapid-response team programs place somewhat more emphasis than New Jersey on employer involvement. In the case of the Arizona Pre-Layoff Assistance Coordination Team (PACT) program, an employer planning a layoff or plant closure initiates the process by alerting state UI or JTPA officials. A PACT team is then assembled, consisting of staff members from the state's JTPA, UI, and ES offices plus representatives from Arizona's regional system of Dislocated Worker Assistance Centers. The employer is asked to designate a lead official to serve as the company's primary contact for the PACT team, to supply an on-site facility for the prelayoff sessions, and to provide two to four hours of paid time off for workers to attend the sessions.

In addition, companies are encouraged to use their informal contacts to help in the placement of affected workers with other employers in the local labor market and to cooperate with the PACT team in putting on a Job Fair. Once a plant has been closed, remaining displaced workers are transferred to the regional Dislocated Worker Assistance Center for additional reemployment services. Information provided by the state indicates that the PACT program of on-site prelayoff assistance has achieved a placement rate of 89 percent.

The South Carolina Rapid Response Team program differs from both the New Jersey and Arizona programs in its strong economic development focus (see OTA 1986:212). As is the case for the other programs, South Carolina's rapid response teams arrange a site visit following notification of a probable or actual plant closing. What is different about the South Carolina program is that if the team's assessment indicates that closure is avoidable, a strategy is formulated that commits the state to providing assistance directly to the employer. Forms of assistance include loan and tax incentive packages; aid in financial management, marketing, and research and development; and programs to retrain workers for jobs using automated equipment. If the closing is deemed inevitable, on the other hand, the team works to find an alternative owner for the plant and to convert the workforce to new employment.

As a final example of the rapid-response team concept, the "outplacement team" initiative of Rhode Island's Dislocated Workers Program perhaps comes the closest to the IAS model of joint labor-management cooperation. To explain the operation of this initiative, Dislocated Workers Program officials have developed a case study of the closing of a plant in Cranston, Rhode Island owned by the Swiss-based Ciba-Geigy Chemical Corporation. The following discussion is based on the case study.[11]

Following the announcement in January 1984 that the Ciba-Geigy plant would be closed by the end of 1985, a joint labor-management outplacement team was formed, consisting of representatives of the Oil, Chemical, and Atomic Workers Union, the company, and state government. The team adopted the following goals for dealing with the adjustments required by the plant closure:

1. company participation in the adjustment process;
2. sensitivity to the company's production obligations;

3. awareness of the relationship between job loss and workers' feelings of disbelief, despair, and, sometimes, depression;

4. understanding by individual workers of their employment options in the context of a career and life plan; and

5. minimizing the time between jobs.

Given the promise of company resources and the pledge of cooperation by the union, state officials on the team played the role of a consultant to company and union team members who jointly had the final say on the services to be offered.

With the luxury of two years of advance notice, the outplacement team was able to plan and implement a sequence of reemployment activities timed to roughly correspond to the phased shutdown of the plant. During the first year, the team sponsored retirement seminars for potential retirees and a series of workshops for workers not contemplating retirement. The workshops included assistance in financial planning, establishing a job objective, conducting job search, and forming job clubs. The team also developed a listing of workers classified by skill to alert other area employers to the availability of Ciba-Geigy employees and conducted individual and group counseling sessions. It is interesting to note that feedback from the counseling sessions indicated a high level of worker interest in the possibility of self-employment. The team responded to this interest by sponsoring an entrepreneurship seminar which led to a contractual arrangement with the state's Small Business Development Center to provide customized assistance to those for whom starting their own business was still a viable option.

The outplacement team continued to operate during 1985 with the initiation of four additional reemployment activities. The first was a two-day "options fair" designed to acquaint workers with available career counseling and retraining options. The team also acknowledged the relatively low levels of formal schooling of many of the older Ciba-Geigy employees by developing a high school equivalency program offered on-site with the cooperation of the Community College of Rhode Island. Later in the year, the team organized workers into job clubs to better equip them to find jobs on their own. The final activity was a two-day Job Fair which brought together 35 potential employers to meet with Ciba-Geigy workers.

The South Carolina and Rhode Island rapid-response team programs pose two important policy questions not yet considered in this monograph. A question raised by the South Carolina program is the desirability of supplying assistance directly to distressed employers to keep existing facilities open and retain jobs, as opposed to the alternative policy of offering reemployment services to workers laid off when a plant closes. The further question posed by the Rhode Island program is the wisdom of assisting unemployed workers to establish their own small businesses. The next chapter briefly treats state economic development initiatives which take the form of packages of financial and other types of assistance to attract new employers, retain old employers, and find new owners for idled facilities. Also considered in chapter 5 are worker ownership initiatives, including employee buyout assistance and British and French experience with unemployed entrepreneur programs.

Summary

Ruth Fedrau, a noted manpower analyst who was instrumental in establishing the California's rapid-response program (the California Economic Adjustment Team), lists seven principles for developing a successful worker reemployment program (see Fedrau 1984). The principles stress the desirability of (1) early notification of layoffs, (2) straightforward communication with employees and union representatives on planned plant closures and available reemployment services, (3) temporary but intensive services preferably located on-site, (4) providing an assistance center on-site, (5) pooling the resources of community organizations and government agencies, (6) providing a wide range of services, and (7) joint management-labor sponsorship of assistance.

This chapter discussed how these principles are implemented in existing reemployment initiatives. The first half of the chapter dealt with the issue of advance notification. Included is an overview of advance notice laws on the books in three states and the federal Worker Adjustment and Retraining Notification Act. The limited empirical evidence currently available on the impact of advance notice on the subsequent unemployment experience of displaced workers is also examined. The empirical evidence suggests that advance notice is effective in speeding up the transition of displaced workers to new jobs, primarily by encouraging workers to locate employment prior to scheduled termination dates. Thus advance notification appears to reduce both the private and social costs of adjustment associated with worker displacement.

What makes advance notice legislation controversial is the question of whether this benefit to workers and to society as a whole is sufficient to offset the private cost to employers of higher fixed costs of employment and the possible negative effect on worker productivity created by such laws. In the absence of evidence demonstrating an adverse effect on employers, most analysts take the position that, on balance, advance notification requirements represent sound social policy.

The latter half of the chapter considered the temporary on-site reemployment programs suggested by the third through seventh of Fedrau's principles. Included in the discussion was the highly regarded Canadian Industrial Assistance Service program. The main strength of the IAS is its encouragement of the active participation by employers in using their informal networks to place workers in jobs that are never publicly announced. The closest U.S. initiative to the IAS is the rapid-response team concept, and the operation of several rapid-response team programs was examined.

In comparison with the IAS, state rapid-response programs differ substantially among themselves in the emphasis placed on employer involvement in minimizing the disruptive effects of displacement. At one end of the spectrum, teams consisting of representatives of relevant state agencies are the dominant players in programs intended to deliver a wide range of reemployment services. Employer participation in these programs tends to be limited to providing time and a place for the on-site delivery of services. At the other extreme, state programs emphasize the joint involvement of management and, where present, unions in locating jobs for displaced workers. In these programs, state officials typically play the more subordinate role of a consultant to the company and union representatives on the team.

NOTES

1. Federal law permits the waiver of the UI work test if the claimant is enrolled in a training program approved by the Employment Security Commissioner of his or her state.

2. The provisions in privately negotiated collective bargaining agreements that provide for advance notice of plant shutdowns are excluded from this discussion.

3. The voluntary Maryland advance notice law passed in 1985 requests that employers of 50 or more workers provide 90 days' notification of permanent layoffs. In addition, employers are requested to continue employee pension and health insurance benefits, and a Quick Response Program to provide on-site assistance to displaced workers was established. As part of its Mature Industries Act, Massachusetts requests employers to give 90 days' advance notification of large layoffs and plant closings and to extend group health insurance coverage to laid-off workers. The Mature Industries Act is discussed in more detail in the next chapter.

4. In a recent decision announced in June 1987 (*Fort Halifax Packing Co. v. Coyne,* No. 86–340), the U.S. Supreme Court ruled that Maine's law requiring one-time severance pay for plant closings does not conflict with federal labor law regulating the administration of employee benefit plans.

5. More common than placement assistance is the offer of either income maintenance of continuation of health insurance. About 45 percent of firms surveyed offered the former, and about 37 percent offered the latter.

6. The 1986 DWS questionnaire poses exactly the same advance notice question as the 1984 questionnaire. This question, as noted in the text, has the serious limitation of confounding the responses of workers who expected to be laid off with the responses of workers who actually received notice of layoff. In the 1988 DWS, the sequence of questions on advance notice is changed so that those who received written notice can be distinguished from those who merely expected to be laid off. A second improvement in the 1988 DWS is access to information on the length of time between the dates of notification and layoff.

7. Hamermesh (1987) notes, however, that the relatively short period of advance notice required in state laws is unlikely to reduce by much the amount of firm-specific investment that is rendered worthless by a plant closing. Indeed, he argues (1987:72) that "[W]hether employers can even be cognizant of impending closings sufficiently far in advance to allow for provision of that information to reduce the costs of adjustment is itself not clear."

8. This legislation added to existing notification requirements the obligation that employers making layoffs must negotiate with employee representatives a "social plan" that specifies compensation to laid-off workers. Moreover, in the event that the two parties cannot agree on the provisions of the social plan, the law provides for binding arbitration.

9. A related on-site vocational training program is the Alabama Industrial Development Training program. Begun in 1971, AIDTraining uses a fleet of 36 mobile training units to locate at the sites of manufacturing firms that have expressed interest in moving to or expanding in Alabama.

10. Topics treated in the job workshops include use of labor market information; employer expectations; how to fill out job applications, write a resume, and interview; self-evaluation of skills, abilities, and aptitudes; and learning to sell oneself to a prospective employer.

11. Fedrau (1984) provides a similar case study of the response of the California Economic Adjustment Team to the 1981 closing of a Mack Truck plant in Hayward, California. State officials chose the Mack Truck closure to define the roles state agencies should play in meeting the needs of displaced workers and to develop a model for local communities to follow. In addition to the cooperation of the United Auto Workers and Mack Truck management, Fedrau points out that noteworthy features of the program included (1) the involvement of local business leaders in helping displaced workers with debt, credit, and mortgage problems, and (2) the opening of an assessment/placement center from which reemployment services were provided.

5
Other Initiatives

Most of the programs discussed in chapters 2 through 4 are primarily intended to ease the transition of workers displaced by a plant closing or mass layoff to new jobs in established enterprises. Chapter 4, in particular, began with a quotation which stressed the advantages of on-site programs in assisting this transition. The same passage from the OTA report (1986:234) goes on to suggest that

> . . . such [on-site] programs fill a special need, which is to serve large numbers of workers with similar skills and work histories who are all dumped on the labor market at once. Even in good times, it is difficult for local labor markets to absorb a great many similar workers at the same time.

Even more difficult than absorbing a large number of displaced workers in good times is the absorption problem when times are bad. Results provided by Podgursky and Swaim (1987c) indicate that local labor market conditions significantly affect duration of joblessness, and it is not uncommon for a major plant closure or mass layoff to take place in a depressed labor market so that few local firms are hiring and those jobs that are available are low-wage positions with little opportunity for advancement. In these circumstances, state policymakers have quite naturally shown an interest in developing economic alternatives to plant closures.

Broadly speaking, state-level initiatives to save jobs by retaining existing employers or attracting new ones fall into one or more of the following categories:

1. customized training programs;
2. grants, low-interest loans, and tax concessions to employers located in depressed communities or other specific geographic areas; and
3. assistance to encourage employee buyouts of existing facilities and start-ups of new small businesses by unemployed workers.

Among these three categories, customized training programs have already been discussed in chapter 2. Initiatives falling under the other two headings are the subject of this chapter. Because several of these initiatives are incorporated in the sweeping displaced worker program provided by Massachusetts, the chapter begins with a discussion of that state's Mature Industries Act. Included is a consideration of state assistance to businesses located in depressed geographic areas termed "enterprise zones." The second major section concerns initiatives intended to stimulate employment growth by encouraging the formation of worker-owned enterprises. A brief summary section concludes the chapter.

Massachusetts' Mature Industries Act

In 1983, the Governor of Massachusetts, Michael S. Dukakis, appointed a blue-ribbon commission to develop a cooperative strategy involving business, labor, and government for stabilizing and possibly expanding the state's manufacturing sector. Based on the report of the commission, the Governor proposed and the Massachusetts legislature passed in 1984 a comprehensive law known as the Mature Industries Act. At the heart of this legislation is a voluntary "social compact" between business and government to work together to cushion the impact of plant closings while attempting to stimulate the growth of manufacturing firms. As part of the social compact, employers are expected to conform to certain voluntary standards of corporate behavior. Specifically, employers are to make a good-faith effort to provide at least 90 days' advance notice of large layoffs and plant closings and to supply health insurance coverage to laid-off workers. In exchange, Massachusetts provides access to state programs offering a variety of forms of assistance to displaced employees and financially troubled firms.

The presidential campaign of Governor Dukakis served to focus national attention on the contribution of programs established by the Mature Industries Act to the state's impressive performance in creating new jobs and its very low unemployment rate. As described by Nelson (1987), the Act is currently serving as a model for legislation being considered by other states.

An Overview of the Act[1]

Probably the most important agency created by the Mature Industries Act is the Massachusetts Industrial Service Program, and a good way to get an overview of the Act's provisions is to examine the broad scope of this umbrella organization. In addition to marketing to employers the Act's social compact, the Program's responsibilities include the following:

1. Overseeing an early warning system.

2. At an employer's request, providing assistance to alleviate the conditions that threaten to cause a large layoff, plant closure, or business failure. Examples of such conditions stated in the Act are outmoded production technologies, loss of markets, and poor management.

3. On the request of a local community adversely affected by a major plant closure or business failure, assisting in finding new uses for idled plants and in fostering job creation in the community.

4. If a mass layoff or plant closure is deemed inevitable, assisting in the effort to secure alternative employment and retraining opportunities for displaced employees. This assistance includes coordinating the delivery of available state and federal reemployment services.

Beginning with the first of these responsibilities, the purpose of the early warning system, as described in chapter 4, is to identify industries and particular firms that are likely to experience large losses in employment, plant closures, or bankruptcy. As part of the social compact between the state and employers, moreover, a firm planning a large layoff or plant closure is to notify the director of the state's Division of Employment Security promptly in order to qualify affected workers for reemployment services. The director's responsibility is to certify that a plant closing or partial closing has or will occur. The Act defines a plant closing as the permanent shutting down of a facility which results in at least 90 percent of the employees being permanently separated within a six-month period prior to the date of certification (the anticipated date of plant closure). A partial closing is the permanent cessation of a "major discrete part of the business" which results in the layoff of a "significant" number of employees and which affects workers and communities in a manner similar to that of a plant closing. Notice of certification is given to the employer as well as to any union or unions representing the employees, and an appeal procedure is available to any party wishing to challenge the certification decision.

Turning to the second and third of the four duties listed, the Act gives a separate quasi-public agency, titled the Economic Stabilization Trust, the responsibility for providing financial assistance to existing or reorganized enterprises in mature industries. The Trust has its own board of trustees, but the director of the Industrial Service Program serves as its chief executive officer; and the Trust is physically located in the central office of the Program. In the language of the Act, "[T]he purpose of the economic stabilization trust shall be to provide flexible high risk financing necessary to implement a change of ownership, a corporate restructuring, or a turnaround plan for an economically viable, but troubled, business. . . ." The Trust is designed to supplement the credit available through private financial institutions and public economic development agencies, but it is specifically instructed not to apply the loan loss standards of private commercial lenders. Rather, the Trust is to consider the social costs of a plant closure or business failure and the tax revenues generated by an ongoing business enterprise.

In addition to the Economic Stabilization Trust, the Act established a second quasi-public funding agency—the Massachusetts Product Development Corporation—intended to operate independently of the Industrial Service Program. The role of the Corporation is to assist economically viable existing firms to increase their market share and expand employment opportunities. More specifically, the Corporation's legal mandate is to provide financial assistance to encourage the development and marketing of new products in situations where such assistance would not otherwise be reasonably available from private lending institutions.

Established by a separate piece of legislation, a third quasi-public funding agency called the Massachusetts Technology Development Corporation specializes in providing seed money and early-stage financing to entrepreneurs in high-technology areas. (In contrast, the Product Development Corporation is a potential source of funds to any Massachusetts firm.) As recently described by Gupta (1987), entrepreneurs use state grants to get high-tech projects off the ground. Once technical feasibility has been demonstrated, the entrepreneur is in a position to raise additional funds from the private venture capital market.

Besides Massachusetts, a number of other states have created programs to supply entrepreneurs with seed and early-stage financing. Among the best known of these are Pennsylvania's Ben Franklin Partnership, Ohio's Thomas Edison Program, and Michigan's comprehensive network of venture capital and seed capital funds. The Ben Franklin and Thomas Edison programs offer fledgling entrepreneurs grants and a link to scientists and engineers employed in major research centers at state universities. A notable feature of Michigan's venture capital program is its enabling legislation passed in 1983 which allows the program to invest in new enterprises up to 5 percent of the state's public employee pension funds. These pension funds were valued at $15 billion in 1988.

Beyond the three programs providing financial assistance, the director of the Industrial Service Program in Massachusetts is authorized under certain conditions to contract with private consultants to (1) assess the viability of an employer in financial difficulty and develop an adjustment strategy that would allow the business to survive or (2) assist in securing new ownership or new management to keep the business in operation. If the decision is made to seek new ownership, priority is given to selling the business either to its employees or to a resident of the state. With respect to a potential employee buyout, the Act directs that ". . . the director shall inform the employees that the business is for sale, inform the employees of their opportunity to purchase the business, and provide the employees with the same assistance in purchasing said business for which other interested buyers may be eligible."

The fourth responsibility of the Industrial Service Program is to assist in providing reemployment services to workers displaced from their jobs by a certified plant closure. Three forms of assistance are specified in the Act. The first of these—the Reemployment Assistance Program—offers a variety of reemployment services, including counseling, placement assistance, and retraining. Combining state funding with federal JTPA Title III funds, the Reemployment Assistance Program operates out of two types of service centers located across the state. "Emergency assistance centers" provide temporary services on-site to workers displaced by a certified plant closing or large layoff. These emergency assistance centers are Massachusetts' version of the state rapid-response team programs discussed in chapter 4. "Worker assistance centers," in contrast, are designed to serve workers in economically distressed areas of the state, particularly areas affected by long-term unemployment problems. Because of their longer-term, community-based focus, the worker assistance centers attempt to reach workers who remain unemployed for lengthy periods of time after the date of a plant closing or mass layoff.

Displaced workers participating in the Reemployment Assistance Program are eligible for two additional benefits: (1) up to 13 weeks of supplemental Reemployment Assistance Benefits and (2) a maximum of three months of health insurance benefits. The Reemployment Assistance Benefits are intended, when added to regular UI benefits, to bring the individual up to 75 percent of his or her previous weekly wage. Benefits are currently subject to a cap of $108 per week, and the benefit period is reduced by one week for each week of advance notification and/or separation pay. The twofold purpose of the supplemental benefits is to help individual workers and their families adjust to a sudden income loss and to put a floor under aggregate purchasing power in communities adversely affected by the loss of large numbers of jobs.

The third form of assistance is a health insurance program which urges, as part of the Act's social compact, that employers extend group health insurance coverage for up to 90 days to workers who would otherwise be ineligible for coverage because of a partial or complete plant shutdown. In the event of a certified plant closing caused by bankruptcy, however, the insurance premium that would have been borne by the employer is paid by a health insurance benefit fund established by the Act. As would be expected, eligibility for the health insurance program is restricted to displaced individuals not covered by the health insurance carried by another family member.[2]

Innovative Features of the Act

There are at least four features of the Massachusetts Mature Industries Act that warrant further examination. This section continues with a discussion of three of these features. They are supplemental unemployment benefits, continuation of health insurance coverage, and assistance to firms located in depressed sections of the state. The fourth innovative feature—encouragement of employee buyouts—is examined in the next section of the chapter.

Supplemental and extended unemployment benefits. Massachusetts appears to be unique among the states in offering unemployed workers a program that supplements UI payments. Among federal programs, the Trade Adjustment Assistance (TAA) program described in chapter 2 supplemented regular UI payments during the 1974–81 period to boost the level of income support to 70 percent of the previous weekly earnings of eligible claimants. As noted in that chapter, TAA legislation passed in 1981 cut back income support to the level of UI payments.

Labor economists have extensively analyzed the relationship between the level of weekly UI benefits and duration of unemployment. In a survey of the literature, Hamermesh (1977:37) reports that his "best" point estimate of the relationship is that a 10 percentage point increase in the gross wage-replacement ratio (the ratio of UI benefits to wages unadjusted by the then nontaxable status of UI benefits) lengthens the duration of insured unemployment by about half a week. A more recent and widely cited study by Moffitt and Nicholson (1982) similarly finds that a 10 percent increase in the net replacement ratio results in an increase of about 0.4 of a week in length of unemployment spells for a sample containing a disproportionate number of exhaustees, and an increase of about 0.8 to 1.0 week for more representative samples.

While Massachusetts is alone in supplementing the level of UI benefits, several states, including California, Connecticut, Alaska, Hawaii, and Puerto Rico, provide state-funded programs extending the length of UI payments. Historically, the maximum duration of UI payments has also varied over time in response to special congressional action and to federal legislation that includes "trigger" mechanisms based on state-insured unemployment rates. The purpose of extended benefits is to provide the income support necessary to allow qualified displaced workers to take advantage of longer, more intensive training courses that cannot readily be squeezed into the usual 26-week maximum duration of UI payments. The main disadvantage of extended benefits is the potential disincentive to return to work. Moffitt and Nicholson report that an increase in maximum duration of one week results in a 0.1 week increase in average weeks unemployed.

Health insurance coverage. Most Americans with health insurance are covered by a group plan for which the employer pays the premium. When a worker's job ends, therefore, insurance coverage generally also terminates, usually within 30 to 60 days. The OTA report (1986:118) points out that individual policies may cost more than twice as much as the group plans they replace.

In a recent article, Podgursky and Swaim (1987a) use 1984 DWS data to examine the extent to which displaced workers are likely to be without health insurance coverage for an extended period of time. They find that for displaced workers who enjoyed group health coverage on their previous jobs, 57.9 percent of blue-collar and 70.1 percent of white-collar and service workers reported that they were currently covered by some sort of group policy. Not surprisingly, the incidence of coverage is strongly associated with employment status. But even for reemployed workers, only 71.0 percent of blue-collar workers and 79.6 percent of white-collar and service workers were covered by a group plan.

Podgursky and Swaim also utilize a second survey administered in 1984—the Work Experience Survey—to examine the extent to which displaced workers who had earlier lost employer group health insurance are covered by other types of health insurance. Their results indicate that many of these workers were able to fall back on coverage from another family member's group policy or on a government health insurance program such as medicaid. Nevertheless, 23.2 percent of blue-collar workers and 16.2 percent of white-collar workers are found to have had no health insurance coverage whatsoever. Worth noting is the fact that these estimates do not include a sizable fraction of workers (8.5 percent and 12.3 percent of blue-collar and white-collar workers, respectively) who reported coverage by some other unspecified type of health insurance policy. The authors note that the comprehensiveness and quality of insurance programs that fall into this residual category are open to question.

In contrast to the provision of supplemental unemployment benefits, the lead taken by Massachusetts in the area of health insurance coverage has been followed by other states. The annual surveys of new state labor legislation provided by Nelson (1984; 1985; 1986; and 1987) suggest that states are taking three different approaches in attempting to extend health insurance coverage to displaced workers. The first approach is to request that employers continue to provide health insurance coverage to displaced workers. This approach is followed in Massachusetts' social compact and in the voluntary guidelines included in Maryland's Economic Stabilization Act.

The second approach taken in recent legislation passed by several other states permits displaced workers, at their own expense, to continue participating in a group health insurance program. Clearly the strongest health insurance provision, however, is that taken in a third approach followed by Connecticut. Connecticut employers of 100 or more workers, who close or relocate, must pay for the continuation of existing group health insurance for affected employees and their dependents for up to 120 days. An Iowa law also spells out specific circumstances under which an employer remains liable for the continuation of benefits to displaced workers.

Enterprise zones. Many states have recently enacted legislation similar to the provisions of the Mature Industries Act intended to stimulate economic development and create jobs in severely depressed areas. The selected depressed areas are commonly known as "enterprise zones." Enterprise zones within a state are geographic areas identified by such factors as high unemployment, a concentration of low-income households, and decreases in population. Within cities, enterprise zones typically include blighted inner-city neighborhoods. Once a zone has been identified, special state services are provided to employers and workers located or residing within the zone. Bendick and Rasmussen (1986) report that 21 states have some form of enterprise zone legislation on their books.

The original formulation of the enterprise zone approach to economic development was modeled after the highly successful experiment in unfettered capitalism in Hong Kong. Advocates of this approach argue that the rapid growth exhibited in a low-income nation like Hong Kong can be attributed, at least in part, to an absence of government regulation and low tax rates. With minimal government presence in the marketplace, individual entrepreneurs enjoy both a strong incentive to work hard and invest and an an opportunity to adapt flexibly to changing economic circumstances. Thus the expected outcome of an enterprise zone policy is a high birth rate of new, small business firms.

The enterprise zone concept was congenial to the supply-side economics approach to economic policy during the early years of the Reagan administration, and President Reagan sent a federal enterprise zone proposal to Congress in 1983. Although the proposed Enterprise Zone Employment and Development Act did not receive Congressional approval, the 1983 legislation is useful in illustrating the specific forms that an enterprise zone policy might take. As described in Weiner (1984), major provisions of the proposed Act are the following:

1. A general payroll tax credit for employers increasing net employment in a zone equal to 10 percent of each additional employee's wage up to a maximum credit per employee of $1,750.

2. A nonrefundable special tax credit equal to 50 percent of the employee's earnings (with no upper limit) for employers hiring disadvantaged individuals in a zone. Disadvantaged workers are defined to include welfare and general assistance recipients.

3. A nonrefundable tax credit for employees working in the zone of 5 percent of the employee's earnings up to a maximum credit per employee of $525.

4. A nonrefundable 3 or 5 percent investment tax credit, over and above the regular investment tax credit, on capital investment in a zone, and a 10 percent credit for the construction or reconstruction of buildings in a zone.

5. Elimination of all long-term capital gains taxes on business property in a zone.

6. Preservation in zones of the use of tax-exempt, small-issue industrial development bonds.

7. Increased regulatory flexibility in zones, whereby federal agencies and regulatory bodies could relax, upon request of state and local authorities, any regulatory requirement except requirements provided by statute or affecting civil rights, safety, or public health.

8. A requirement that state and local governments commit themselves to specific actions to enhance development of a zone, including tax and regulatory relief, improved services, and community involvement.

The employment tax credits included in the first through the third of these provisions represent a wage subsidy intended to encourage employers to supply more OJT opportunities. Because the tax credits are mainly nonrefundable and capital-raising provisions are largely absent, Weiner points out that the proposal would be expected to be effective in inducing existing zone firms to expand and nonzone firms to open new branches in the zone, but relatively less effective in promoting the birth of small businesses. The major reasons are that (1) small firms are unlikely to be profitable enough to benefit from the nonrefundable tax credits, and (2) one of the chief obstacles facing potential entrepreneurs is the need to raise capital. As will be described in more detail in the next section, small business creation is often seen as a crucial factor in encouraging economic development and growth in employment opportunities. Also worth noting in connection with the seventh provision is the meager attempt at achieving greater regulatory flexibility.

With the defeat of President Reagan's enterprise zone proposal in Congress, Bendick and Rasmussen (1986:114–18) point out that the role of the states has become central to the implementation of the zone idea. Their summary of existing state programs indicates the following general patterns. First, most states focus on tax incentive efforts with little more than a nod in the direction of regulatory flexibility. Second, most of the tax incentives are straightforward reductions of total tax burdens, as opposed to reductions in marginal tax rates designed to increase work effort or entrepreneurial initiative. Finally, most states are supplementing their tax incentives with extensive government activity within zones. Examples of these activities are land use planning, infrastructure development, improvement of public services, loan funds, technical assistance, and the training of disadvantaged workers.

Because of problems including inadequate or inappropriate incentives, lack of coordination with other state programs, and excessive red tape, Bendick and Rasmussen also note that a number of states are planning to seek major revisions of their initial enterprise zone legislation. These revisions may well embody a return to the original enterprise zone concept with its emphasis on the birth and development of small, indigenous firms.

In this connection, state-funded "incubator" programs represent an initiative already in operation in a number of states which is specifically intended to "hatch" new small businesses. Incubators are generally defined as multi-tenant buildings offering affordable space and a variety of support systems to start-up companies. Describing the 31 small business incubators located in Pennsylvania, former Governor Richard Thornburgh (1988:5) writes that the buildings housing the start-ups

> . . . range from an empty apparel manufacturing facility, now housing two fledgling electronic businesses previously operating out of the proverbial basement and garage, to the former Bethlehem Steel Homer Research Center in the Lehigh Valley. The latter has been crammed with over 20 new and diversified small businesses (including one that operated for a time out of the facility's former coat closet).

Support systems typically provided in incubators include shared office services such as telephone answering and word processing; the professional assistance of lawyers, accountants, and management consultants; and access to capital. The objective of an incubator is to nurture the growth of fledgling companies by making it possible for entrepreneurs to concentrate their energies on producing the product or service on which the survival of the business depends. Also important to the growth of incubator firms is the informal support system that often develops as tenants overcome early crises and become familiar with each other's operations.

Worker Ownership Initiatives

The overview of the enterprise zone concept in the previous section emphasized policy initiatives designed to provide an environment in which employers located in depressed areas are encouraged to maintain or even expand the employment opportunities they offer. This section shifts to a discussion of initiatives directed at stimulating employment growth by encouraging the formation of worker-owned enterprises. Two types of initiatives are considered. The first includes programs providing assistance to enable employee groups to save their jobs by purchasing companies or facilities that might otherwise close. The second includes assistance to individual unemployed workers to help them start up their own small businesses.

Employee Buyout Programs

Returning for a moment to the Massachusetts Mature Industries Act, the director of the Division of Employment Security is instructed, in the case of a plant closure, to inform affected employees that the business is for sale and that they have an opportunity to purchase the facility with the same assistance that would be offered to any other potential buyer. As described earlier, financial assistance provided by the Economic Stabilization Trust is available for implementing a change in ownership of a business that is financially troubled but is nevertheless considered economically viable.

Over the 1981–85 period, Balderston (1986:24) reports that a total of 14 states, including Massachusetts, enacted legislation specifically promoting employee ownership. More recently, Nelson (1986; 1987) indicates that three additional states have passed laws to assist the development of employee-owned firms. Most of these laws authorize programs that offer a combination of technical and financial assistance to employee groups seeking to purchase a business that would otherwise close. One example is the 1984 Pennsylvania Employee-Ownership Assistance Program, which appropriated $15 million over three years to promote the restructuring of existing businesses, including those facing layoffs or closings, into employee-owned enterprises. Approximately $3 million of this total was to be spent in providing technical assistance to employee groups considering the employee buyout option, and the remaining $12 million was intended to assist in the financing of employee buyouts.

A second example—the 1986 Michigan Employee-Owned Corporation Act—is interesting in terms of the specificity of the services provided employee groups wishing to develop an employee-owned corporation. As described in Nelson (1987), the state's Labor Department is directed to assist in the formation or operation of employee-owned corporations by (1) developing and disseminating information on procedures for carrying out an employee buyout; (2) evaluating the feasibility and economic viability of proposed employee-owned corporations; (3) providing technical assistance and counseling services; (4) assisting in obtaining financing; (5) coordinating local, state, federal, and private agency assistance; and (6) recommending appropriate legislative or executive action to enhance opportunities for such corporations. With respect to financing, the law specifically states that employee-owned corporations are to be considered eligible for grants and loans provided by the state's Public Economic Development Corporation to assist businesses to locate and expand in Michigan.[3]

As a final example, the New Jersey Employee Stock Ownership Plan Act of 1984 is worth noting because it spells out a methodology to be used in determining whether an enterprise is economically viable. The Act directs that when a plant closure is anticipated or actually takes place in an already economically distressed municipality, the Commissioner of Commerce and Economic Development may fund the preparation of a cost-benefit analysis of the potential profitability of an employee buyout. After a review of the results of the analysis, financial assistance including loan guarantees or low-interest loans is to be provided to employee purchasers if the benefits are judged to exceed the costs and funds are available.

State initiatives designed to encourage employee buyouts of troubled firms reflect the general interest in employee ownership which has developed over the past 10 to 15 years. It appears that this interest, in turn, largely stems from two factors: (1) the series of tax incentives embodied in Employee Stock Ownership Plans (ESOPs), and (2) evidence from case studies of a favorable impact on labor productivity and profits of greater worker participation in decisionmaking.

Focusing on the first of these factors, an ESOP is a corporate finance strategy used to provide company stock to employees on a tax-favored basis. The way it works is that the company sets up a special trust similar to a pension or profit-sharing trust to which it contributes shares of its own stock. Stock held in the trust is allocated to the accounts of individual employees, making them partial owners of the company. In a typical ESOP, employees receive an amount of stock equivalent to 5 to 15 percent of their annual compensation. Thus while employees may make wage and benefit concessions to permit a failing firm to survive (including, in some cases, giving up their pension plans in return for an equity stake in the company), only rarely do employees groups directly borrow to purchase company stock.

A major tax advantage of the formation of an ESOP is that the value of stock contributions made by the employer is tax deductible from the company's income. In 1984, Congress made ESOPs even more attractive when it permitted lenders to deduct from taxable income 50 percent of the interest earned on ESOP loans, thus making it possible for lenders to profit while lending to ESOPs at below-market rates. Tax reform legislation passed in 1986 also permits an ESOP using stock dividends to repay debt to deduct the dividends from its tax liability.

Rosen, Klein, and Young (1986:15) point out that as of 1984 there were over 7,000 ESOP plans in existence, covering over 10 million employees. As they note, ESOPs are established for a variety of reasons. These reasons include improving employee benefits, raising capital cheaply, making a market for the sale of the equity position of a departing owner, implementing a participatory management philosophy, carrying out a leveraged buyout (i.e., a buyout in which management or outside investors borrow enough money to buy a controlling interest in the firm), and enabling employees to buy out a firm that would otherwise close. Employee buyouts of failing companies represent the most publicized of the uses of ESOPs, even though it is one of the least common. Most companies become employee-owned as part of a business strategy to restructure the ownership of an ongoing firm. Indeed, Kuttner (1985a:20) remarks that ". . . most examples of 'employee ownership' are still cases of traditional corporate management recognizing the value of making the workplace a bit less alienating, rather than workers effectively organizing production."

Turning to the case study evidence, probably the best known example of a favorable impact of worker ownership on productivity and profits is the case of Weirton Steel. In March 1982, Weirton's then parent, the National Steel Corporation, announced that it planned to close its mill located in the small town of Weirton, West Virginia. The mill was only marginally profitable, and National Steel was rapidly diversifying away from primary metals. The closing of the mill would have meant the loss of over 7,000 jobs and the possible death of the community.

Following a year and a half of negotiations and exhaustive preparation based on an ESOP master plan developed by a well-known consulting firm, an employee buyout of the mill was worked out in which workers agreed to a 20 percent reduction in wages and benefits. Moreover, worker compensation was frozen at the new lower level for six years and employees had to wait five years to receive full voting rights.

Since the buyout was completed in January 1984, Weirton Steel has survived and even prospered to the extent that the company has reported 13 consecutive profitable quarters and has hired back all 3,000 workers formerly on layoff. While worker wage and benefit concessions clearly played a role in Weirton's success, O'Boyle and Roth (1985) also emphasize the importance of breaking down old antagonisms between management and labor, increasing employee participation at all levels of decisionmaking within the firm, and establishing a profit-sharing plan.

It must be pointed out, however, that the success thus far of Weirton Steel is not necessarily representative of all attempts at employee buyouts. A case in point is the failure of worker ownership at the Rath Packing Company, a meat-packing firm located in Waterloo, Iowa. Hammer and Stern (1986) describe how the threat of Rath's closure in 1978 led the local union to negotiate an employee buyout effected in 1980. Through an ESOP, employees gained 60 percent of the company's stock and majority representation on the board of directors, as well as a commitment from the firm to give workers at all levels involvement in decisionmaking. For their part, workers agreed to defer improvements in wages and benefits called for by the packing industry's master contract.

While the shop-floor productivity committees established by the ESOP initially appeared to work well, pressures exerted by a traditionally adversarial labor-management relationship and continued financial losses led to management demands for further worker wage and benefit concessions and to union demands for personnel changes in top management. By the spring of 1983, union leaders had abandoned the system of shop-floor committees, and open conflict was breaking out over conditions of work and company finances. The company ultimately filed in November 1983 for protection under Chapter 11 of the bankruptcy code.

The Rath Packing Company experience highlights some of the risks involved in an employee buyout of a failing firm. Recent discussions of the use of ESOPs as a financing tool (see, for example, Kotlowitz and Bean 1987) also raise questions about the actual benefits to workers. One problem is that ESOPs have to be highly leveraged to take full advantage of tax breaks, since these breaks are debt-related. This makes ESOPs especially vulnerable to an economic downturn. Other concerns are that workers often receive only a passive role in company decision-making and that workers are obliged to shoulder greater risk when stock ownership is substituted for conventional pension plans.[4]

In addition to case study evidence, there are also a limited number of empirical studies relating to the effect of employee ownership on labor productivity and the job creation performance of firms. Rosen and Klein (1983) report on a survey carried out by the National Center for Employee Ownership (NCEO) of the structural characteristics and employment growth of majority employee-owned companies. Over the 1977–82 period, the 43 employee-owned firms included in the survey are found to have averaged an annual employment growth rate 2.78 percentage points higher than that of conventional firms in the same economic sectors. The authors point out that over a 10-year period this difference means that employee-owned firms would generate 31 percent more jobs than comparable conventional firms.

A subsequent NCEO survey described by Rosen, Klein, and Young (1986) collected data for 37 ESOP companies and 2,804 employees. The purpose of the survey was to investigate the relationship between employees' satisfaction with their jobs and their employers and such ESOP characteristics as the percentage of company stock owned by the ESOP, worker voting rights, and the reason the company established its ESOP. The authors find that ESOPs can function effectively to motivate workers and increase job satisfaction if employers (1) are willing to make significant financial contributions to the plan, (2) are strongly committed to the philosophy of employee ownership, and (3) are ready to develop an active program to educate employees about the ESOP. It is interesting to note from the Rosen, Klein, and Young study that the reason a company established its ESOP appears to have no effect on the employee satisfaction variables.

Besides ESOPs, worker cooperatives are the other major form of employee ownership. A recent empirical study by Jones (1987) uses data for a 1978 sample of 50 British retail cooperatives to obtain econometric estimates of the effect on labor productivity of worker financial participation and employee involvement in decisionmaking through representation on boards of directors. His results indicate that board representation has a positive impact on productivity, especially the presence of worker-directors who currently are employed or once were employed in the same co-op. On the other hand, financial participation by employees negatively impacts productivity. Jones notes that the latter finding is the opposite of what is typically found for producer co-ops. For example, Jones and Svejnar (1985) report for a large sample of Italian producer cooperatives that profit-sharing and worker ownership of assets as well as worker participation in management tend to increase productivity. Jones (1987) notes that this difference may reflect the low level of financial participation by employees in retail co-ops as compared to producer co-ops. For retail co-ops, the net impact on labor productivity of both forms of worker participation is small but positive.

Unemployed Entrepreneur Programs

Although initiatives to assist unemployed workers to become self-employed have yet to be implemented in permanent programs in this country, U.S. policymakers are presently showing a strong interest in the unemployed entrepreneur concept. An example is the useful USDOL (1986) report prepared at the request of Senators Gary Hart, Bob Packwood, and Lloyd Bentsen, who expressed a particular interest in the potential for allowing UI benefits to be used to help support unemployed workers in the start-up phase of establishing their own small businesses.

Following up on this interest, the USDOL entered into a cooperative agreement with Washington state in the fall of 1987 to fund a demonstration project to test the effectiveness of making UI benefits available to claimants who establish small businesses. Approximately 400 laid-off workers were to be provided an incentive to start their own business by the offer of lump-sum payments of up to $6,000. Since the demonstration project was to be funded by the federal government, it would not violate the federal ban restricting states from paying UI benefits to unemployed workers not actively engaged in job search. Galante (1987) also notes that the states of Michigan, New Jersey, and Massachusetts are studying ways of using UI benefits to help unemployed workers in launching new businesses.

Support for unemployed entrepreneur programs appears to represent the convergence of two considerations. The first is evidence initially presented by Birch (1981) showing that small firms create many more jobs than large companies. A widely cited finding of his study is that of all the net new jobs created between 1969 and 1976, two-thirds were generated by firms with 20 or fewer employees, and about 80 percent were created by firms with 100 or fewer employees. These proportions are far higher than the share of total employment represented by small businesses.[5] At the same time, the USDOL report (1986:58) presents evidence to show that many independent small businesses are successful attempts at self-employment. The second consideration is the persistent argument that, given the adjustment problems faced by displaced workers, expenditure of UI funds for programs other than its traditional income maintenance role ought to be explored.

Several major European countries have established programs permitting the diversion of transfer payments to unemployed workers who commit themselves to starting their own small businesses. Two of the best known of these programs were established in France in 1979 and in the United Kingdom in 1982.[6] The French Unemployed Entrepreneurs Program provides a lump-sum payment to be received about two months after the new firm has been registered. (Benefits may also be used to buy an existing business.) The size of the payment was initially determined by the worker's previous unemployment insurance contributions subject to a cap of six months of unemployment benefits. Since April 1984, the range of payments has been narrowed by making payment size vary only according to the length of unemployment (the sooner after losing a job the worker starts his or her business, the larger the benefits) and the type of benefit the recipient was previously receiving. Bendick and Egan (1987:530) report that payments currently range in dollar terms between $1,398 and $5,590. In addition to the lump-sum payment, program participants receive a payment for each job created beyond that occupied by the proprietor. Before April 1984, the French program was funded through the unemployment insurance trust fund, and since then it has been funded by general tax revenues.

Rather than a lump-sum payment, the British Enterprise Allowance Scheme provided a taxable allowance equivalent to $61 per week in 1983 for a maximum of 52 weeks. Program participants must have been without work for at least eight weeks, must be willing to work at the business full time, and must demonstrate that they have at least 1000 British pounds ($1,520 in 1983) to invest in the business. Only new businesses are eligible for assistance. As is the case for the French program, an assessment of the viability of the proposed business is not part of the application review process,[7] and the program is funded by general tax revenues. Both programs also provide limited training and technical assistance to would-be entrepreneurs.

The fact that the programs in both France and Britain have survived for a number of years is an important measure of success for this type of initiative. Nevertheless, recent evaluations by Bendick and Egan (1987) and the USDOL (1986) raise several questions regarding the potential of unemployed entrepreneur programs for returning the unemployed to work and creating additional jobs. These questions include the following:

1. How many new firms would have been created in the absence of assistance?

2. Might the subsidized firms compete against and displace existing firms in the same local markets?

3. How good are the jobs self-employment provides?

4. How many jobs do these firms generate in addition to those held by their proprietors?

Beginning with the first question, by the end of 1985 about 235,000 persons had participated in the French program and about 139,000 in the British. The programs involve only a fraction of 1 percent of the annual flow of unemployment in both countries, yet 20 to 30 percent of new business starts are program-generated. Without a formal evaluation including a control group comparison, it is difficult to say how many of the business starts would have taken place in the absence of the programs. The only available evidence on this question is a 1985 survey of Enterprise Allowance Scheme participants. As described by

Bendick and Egan (1987:530–31), 33.5 percent of participants surveyed reported that they would have established their businesses at the same time without the program, and an additional 17.2 percent said that they would have gone ahead but with some delay. Thus about half of the new firms formed in the U.K. might have occurred without program assistance.

The absence of formal evaluation also makes it difficult to provide a definitive answer to the second question. Nevertheless, it does appear likely that displacement of existing firms by subsidized firms will occur. One piece of evidence comes from the 1985 survey of British program participants. The relevant question asked proprietors of subsidized firms for an estimate of the extent to which their firm's sales took business from other firms, as opposed to offering products or services not previously available. Two-thirds of the responding proprietors said that displacement accounted for less than 10 percent of their sales. The remaining one-third reported that displacement accounted for 11 to 100 percent of sales. Based on this survey, Bendick and Egan (1987:535) note that the British government's estimate of worker displacement is that one worker is thrown into unemployment for every two employed.

Also related to the displacement question is a consideration of the location and product lines of newly established businesses. The fact that most proprietors are able to make only a modest front-end financial investment in their businesses limits the choice of activity undertaken. Thus subsidized firms are predominantly involved in the services and retail trade industries, so that they are dependent on local consumers and the level of local income. Both of these industries tend to be highly competitive, with the product or service of one firm a close substitute for that of other firms. To the extent that prospective entrepreneurs reside in depressed areas and communities, in addition, the local demand for goods and services is likely to be quite limited.

Turning to the question of the quality of jobs that self-employment provides, summary statistics indicate for the British program that median earnings (about $8,000 annually) and the distribution of earnings for program participants are about the same as their market alternatives would have provided. These statistics are calculated for firms that survived three years. But how likely are small enterprises to survive this long? The experience in Europe as well as in the U.S. is that small businesses generally have a high failure rate. For the French program specifically, about one-third of newly formed firms ceased operation within their first three years. A similar failure rate is estimated for Enterprise Allowance Scheme firms.

Even if a subsidized business should fail, it might be argued that the program is still worthwhile if it increases the probability that former proprietors will find jobs with existing employers. For the British program, however, Bendick and Egan (1987:536) conclude that the flow into employment of proprietors of failed businesses is not observably higher than the flow estimated for all male unemployed workers. Strengthening their conclusion is the fact that program participants have somewhat better credentials, and therefore a better chance of reemployment, than the average unemployed workers.

The final question concerns the job-creating performance of subsidized small businesses. Does their performance live up to the high rate of job creation said to be characteristic of new small firms? The answer seems to be that only a small subset of subsidized firms are likely to provide employment opportunities in addition to the job held by the proprietor. For the British program, 62 percent of businesses still operating after three years supplied employment only for the proprietor, and only 5 percent employed more than six persons. Parallel results are reported for the Unemployed Entrepreneurs Program. It should be noted, moreover, that these percentages include part-time workers and family members who may or may not be paid.

In summary, both the USDOL and Bendick-Egan studies offer a less-than-enthusiastic recommendation for transferring the unemployed entrepreneur initiative to this country. The USDOL report (1986:63) expresses two main concerns. The first is that given the higher incidence of self-employment in the U.S. than in Europe, payments to program participants are likely to represent a windfall in the sense that benefits are paid to persons who would have taken the desired action in the absence of the program. The second concern is that subsidies that induce start-ups by unemployed persons with no previous entrepreneurial experience and little initial capital to invest may exacerbate the already high rate of small business failure.

For similar reasons, Bendick and Egan (1987:541) conclude that ". . . grant diversion for small business development should be at most a minor component of the spectrum of efforts to promote employment opportunities for the hard-to-employ." A minor role for grant diversion follows from the widespread agreement that the forms of assistance most needed by newly created small businesses are counseling and financial assistance. Moreover, Bendick and Egan point out that unemployed entrepreneur programs are subject to the same trade-off as that facing traditional reemployment initiatives; namely, the trade-off between serving the hardest-to-employ and achieving high success rates for program participants.

Reinforcing the recommendation of a limited role for unemployed entrepreneur programs is the experience gained from a small pilot project in Ohio designed to test the effectiveness of self-employment training. This project was operated during the 1985–86 period by the Ohio Bureau of Employment Services using JTPA Title III funds. All 200 displaced workers participating in the project received formal training in skills thought to be related to entrepreneurial success as well as post-program support services. Across the seven program providers, program content ranged from courses in basic business skills such as accounting, market research, and personnel selection to seminars stressing motivation and esteem building.

The analysis of the Ohio pilot project by Mangum and Tansky (1987) indicates that 31 percent of participants actually started a small business, but less than 10 percent of all participants successfully created businesses that offered much chance of generating employment opportunities for others and of providing predisplacement levels of earnings. Average program cost per small business start-up was $6,767. The authors conclude that displaced workers most likely to start businesses with a reasonable probability of survival had substantial savings or equity in their homes, possessed some managerial experience from previous employment, and had been displaced for a relatively short time. Self-employment training thus appears to be a viable option for only a very select group within the displaced worker population.

Summary

In contrast to the vocational training and JSA programs discussed in
earlier chapters, this chapter described a number of less conventional
initiatives for assisting displaced workers by developing economic alternatives to plant closures and by encouraging small business start-ups.
Since several of these initiatives are incorporated in the comprehensive Massachusetts Mature Industries Act, the chapter began with an
outline of the Act, including the voluntary "social compact" it establishes
between business and government to cushion the adverse employment
impacts of plant closings. A unique feature of the Massachusetts displaced worker program is the provision of supplemental unemployment
benefits for a period not to exceed 13 weeks. Other adjustment assistance
initiatives offered by Massachusetts, as well as by other states, include
continuation of health insurance coverage for displaced workers and
"enterprise zone" programs providing special government assistance
and tax relief to employers located in distressed areas of the state.

The second half of the chapter dealt with programs intended to retain jobs and stimulate employment growth by encouraging the formation of employee-owned enterprises. These programs typically take one
of two forms: (1) assisting employee groups to purchase facilities that
would otherwise be closed, and (2) assistance to enable individual
unemployed workers to start up their own small businesses. The discussion of the first type of program focused on case studies of Weirton
Steel and the Rath Packing Company and on a handful of empirical
studies relating to the impact of ESOPs on worker productivity and job
creation. While the available evidence is not terribly persuasive one
way or the other, it does appear that under certain conditions a case
can be made for public assistance in worker buyout attempts.

The second type of worker-ownership program was primarily discussed in terms of the experience in Britain and France with national
unemployed entrepreneur programs. Programs in both countries have
been viewed as sufficiently successful that their funding has been continued over time. In neither case, however, is quantitative evidence
available allowing a comparison of the performance of program participants with that of a control group. Even in the absence of experimental

data, however, important questions were raised from the available evidence regarding the ability of most displaced workers to start up a viable small business and the limited potential for job creation in addition to the job of the proprietor. Caution is thus warranted in recommending the extension of this type of program to the U.S.

NOTES

1. This discussion is primarily based on the enabling legislation for the Mature Industries Act and the legislative report of the state Division of Employment Security (1987).

2. An interesting third case covered by the Act is that the state health insurance benefit fund will pay for continued coverage by health insurance policies individually purchased by workers displaced by a certified plant closing.

3. As described in Trolin and Randall (1987), another interesting funding initiative, included in the proposed Oregon Employee Ownership Act, would allow employees to use their UI benefits to purchase shares in companies that would otherwise close down.

4. On the other hand, Miller (1988) points out that, as shareholders, workers may enjoy substantial windfall gains when an ESOP-owned firm is taken public or sells out in a transaction that eventually reduces or eliminates employee ownership. Ironically, this outcome flouts congressional intent (i.e., the encouragement of worker ownership) in giving tax-favored treatment to ESOPs.

5. Wessel and Brown (1988) offer an interesting discussion of various criticisms of the thesis that small businesses generate nearly all of U.S. job growth and report Birch's response to his critics.

6. The discussion of these two programs relies heavily on the data presented and analyzed in Bendick and Egan (1987).

7. While a screening of business proposals would be likely to decrease failures, program officials in both countries have been reluctant to adopt a policy of extensive screening. One reason is the additional program cost and complexity associated with screening. A second factor is a reluctance to substitute the judgment of agency personnel for that of the entrepreneur and the market.

6
Summary and Policy Implications

The introductory chapter of this study posed six major questions involving the provision of effective labor market adjustment assistance to displaced workers. Chapters 2 through 5 then described a variety of specific initiatives through which assistance is or could be supplied. The focus in these chapters was on contemporary, innovative, state-level programs. Available quantitative and qualitative evidence on these programs was also presented in detail.

The first section of this concluding chapter attempts to answer each of the six questions. The purpose of the question-and-answer format is to be as concrete as possible in spelling out what can be learned from state, federal, and, in a few cases, foreign government experience about how best to cope with the adjustment problems faced by displaced workers. A second section briefly outlines what appears to be the best mix of displaced worker programs.

Major Policy Questions

Question 1: How do displaced workers differ from other unemployed workers?

Adjustment assistance programs directed specifically toward displaced workers are based on the premise that the displaced are different from other unemployed workers in ways that require special services. Not all analysts agree on exactly how to define displaced workers. Nor is there unanimity on the proposition that the displaced worker problem has recently become more serious. Nevertheless, most observers seem to agree that relative to other unemployed workers, displaced workers (1) possess a stable employment history with their predisplacement employers, (2) have little chance of being recalled to jobs with their old employer or in their old industry, and (3) may face poor reemployment prospects in their local labor markets.

An implication of the first difference is that the job search skills of many displaced workers have grown rusty because they had not been obliged to seek alternative employment for a number of years. The length of their unemployment spells is thus likely to be longer than otherwise would be the case. Output foregone because of unnecessary delays in the reemployment process represents a social loss which must be considered in addition to the private losses borne by individual displaced workers and their families.

Evidence from the 1984 Displaced Worker Survey reported in table 1.1 indicates that about 40 percent of workers displaced from their jobs between 1979 and 1984 were unemployed or no longer in the labor force at the end of the survey period, and that nearly half of the displaced workers who drew UI benefits during the 1979–84 period exhausted their eligibility for benefits (i.e., they were unemployed for longer than 26 weeks). The 1986 DWS shows that even with the cyclical upswing in the economy between 1984 and 1986, fully one-third of workers displaced during the 1981–86 period were without employment in January 1986.

The further analysis of 1984 DWS data by Podgursky and Swaim (1987c) shows that the distribution of completed spells of joblessness is highly skewed to the right. While nearly half of respondents in their sample found jobs within 14 weeks of displacement, a substantial minority of displaced workers faced a high risk of being jobless for a year or more. The highly skewed distribution of completed spells makes the average length of unemployment substantially longer than can be reasonably accounted for by cyclical phenomenon or by job search factors such as an unrealistically high initial reservation wage. It also suggests that reemployment programs should be targeted to the minority of workers facing the most severe adjustment problems. Drawing on the Podgursky-Swaim regression results, these individuals include workers displaced from blue-collar occupations, workers with below-average levels of education, minorities and women, and residents of communities with above-average unemployment rates.

The second difference between displaced and other unemployed workers implies that the reemployment of the displaced is likely to involve a change in occupation, industry, or both. Such changes, in turn, often imply lower earnings upon reemployment, which compound the private costs associated with a spell of unemployment. As emphasized in chapter 1, lower earnings arise because a displaced worker (1) received an economic rent on his or her predisplacement job or (2) was forced to forego the opportunity to earn a return on investments previously made in firm-specific human capital. Data compiled from the 1984 DWS and the 1986 DWS indicate that about 30 percent of those reemployed in full-time wage and salary jobs suffered pay cuts of 20 percent or more (see table 1.1). Losses in the form of group health insurance coverage and vested pension plans add to the private costs borne by displaced workers.

In an effort to distinguish between these two explanations of earnings losses, Podgursky and Swaim (1987b) use industry unionization coverage of last job as a proxy measure of the possibility that the predisplacement job provided a significant economic rent. Controlling for this measure as well as predisplacement earnings, the authors find for blue-collar males that a change in industry significantly depresses reemployment earnings, thus providing support for the specific training explanation. Greater tenure on the old job and the area unemployment rate also significantly increase the earnings loss estimated for blue-collar men. On the other hand, years of schooling completed—which can be interpreted as a measure of general training—is found to have a strong positive effect on postdisplacement earnings. Hamermesh (1987) provides further evidence indicating that displacement is not typically anticipated by affected workers and that the value of workers' share of lost returns on firm-specific training can be substantial.

Uncompensated losses on specific training result in a social loss if risk-averse workers and their employers are discouraged from making optimal levels of investment in specific human capital. Even evidence of losses of economic rents can be used to justify special assistance to displaced workers on the grounds that such assistance is politically necessary for the maintenance of a dynamic and open domestic economy.

The third difference between displaced workers and other unemployed workers recognizes that a major plant closure or permanent layoff has a serious impact on employment opportunities in the community. The ripple effect of a closure generates displacement in smaller firms that service the closed establishment and in retail outlets that depend on the purchasing power of laid-off workers. This increases the competition for those jobs that are still available in the local labor market, even though many of them are likely to be low-wage positions offering little opportunity for advancement. Moreover, declining property values and an eroding tax base leaves schools and other public services underfunded, making it even more difficult to attract new employers to the community.

Question 2: Which forms of adjustment assistance "work" for displaced workers?

Just as displaced workers can conceptually be distinguished from other unemployed workers, displaced workers are themselves a heterogeneous population with different backgrounds and skills and with a variety of needs for adjustment assistance. The most highly publicized segment of the displaced worker population includes workers laid off from unionized, high-wage jobs in the manufacturing sector. Many of these workers have made substantial investments in firm-specific training which now must be written off. Others undoubtedly enjoyed sizable rents on their predisplacement jobs.

In spite of the common denominator of having been laid off from a high-paying job in manufacturing, appropriate forms of adjustment assistance may differ substantially for different individuals, even within this group of displaced workers. Some workers may require retraining to qualify for jobs in expanding industries. Many others will benefit from counseling and other types of job search assistance to help them realize that their chances of recall are low but that employment options offering greater career opportunities do exist, albeit at lower wages, in other industries or occupations. For still others in this group, remedial education is a prerequisite before they can be either retrained or assisted in formulating a job search strategy.

It is also important to recognize that the population of displaced workers includes nonunion workers laid off from low-wage jobs in industries other than manufacturing. This group of displaced workers includes individuals who are poorly educated, female, and black or Hispanic. Since these individuals may never have had a chance to accumulate specific human capital, appropriate adjustment services include remedial education and retraining programs intended to provide basic and job-related skills. These programs accompanied by job search assistance offer the potential for enhancing workers' employment opportunities in better-paying occupations.

In response to the variety of needs of displaced workers, states have established a broad spectrum of reemployment assistance programs. As described in chapters 2 through 4, these programs include a number of variants of retraining and job search assistance programs. Still other state programs described in chapter 5 are aimed at maintaining employment opportunities in the local labor market either by enabling current owners to stay in business or by helping to find new owners (including employee groups) to keep existing facilities from closing. Also considered in chapter 5 is the European experience with programs that assist unemployed workers to start their own small businesses. The most important single gap in the spectrum of state programs appears to be in the area of remedial education, a not surprising result given the emphasis of most states on economic development rather than human capital investment.

The rich set of state-level programs provides an opportunity for researchers to pull together and analyze an enormous amount of information about the design and effectiveness of adjustment assistance services. Such information should be invaluable to decisionmakers charged with allocating funds across existing programs, initiating new programs, and terminating old programs. Unfortunately, relatively few state programs have been designed to allow the kind of evaluation which would allow their effectiveness to be measured quantitatively by a comparison of the behavior of individuals randomly assigned to treatment and control groups. Fortunately, there are a few key random-assignment experiments that represent exceptions to this statement.

One of the most important of these exceptions is the Worker Adjustment Demonstration, involving about 2,250 Title III JTPA program participants at three sites located in Houston and El Paso, Texas. Reemployment services randomly assigned to participants in two treatment groups are job search assistance (JSA) and JSA plus referral, where necessary, to a retraining program. Also randomly assigned were the members of a control group who received all available non-Title III services. As described by Bloom and Kulik (1986), WAD participants are found to experience a short-run positive impact on earnings and likelihood of employment, and a corresponding negative impact on UI benefits received. The primary program effect for men is to expedite their reemployment, while for women it appears that wages as well are positively affected by program participation. A surprising result is that the extra cost of retraining services provided to male participants in Houston did not result in additional labor market benefits. The authors suggest that the most realistic explanation for this finding is that a mismatch occurred between the training opportunities offered by the Houston program and the interests and backgrounds of program participants.

The findings of the WAD projects regarding the relative effectiveness of JSA and retraining services are buttressed by results obtained from two federally-funded projects—the Downriver dislocated worker project and the Buffalo project of the national Dislocated Worker Demonstration. Both projects permit a comparison of the outcomes for treatment and control groups, although neither involved random assignment.

All participants in the Downriver project were required to participate in a JSA program and about 60 percent of participants also were enrolled in classroom training. The evaluation report by Kulik, Smith, and Stromsdorfer (1984) indicates that the program significantly improved workers' reemployment rates and postlayoff weekly earnings. It also increased their access to retraining opportunities. However, program training is not found to yield a significant incremental gain in participants' employment prospects above that resulting from JSA services only. Kulik, Smith, and Stromsdorfer qualify this negative finding by noting problems of small sample sizes and the absence of random assignment of workers to training as opposed to JSA.

Like the Downriver project, all participants in the Buffalo program were provided JSA services and about 45 percent also went through a classroom training or OJT program. Despite the low rate of participation (less than 20 percent of displaced workers recruited for the program chose to participate), Corson, Long, and Maynard (1985) report that the program had a favorable effect on the proportion of time spent in the labor force, the proportion of time employed, and average weekly earnings. Among the three main program services, JSA and classroom training are estimated to have impacts of about the same size on workers' labor market experience. In view of the substantially higher cost of classroom training, only JSA services thus appear to be cost effective. Corson, Long, and Maynard note, however, that many classroom training participants completed their training near the end of the demonstration period and consequently received relatively little placement assistance. Interestingly, on-the-job training is not found by the authors to have a discernible impact on employment.

The reemployment bonus concept is another important labor market initiative for which evidence is available from random-assignment experiments. As discussed in chapter 3, results from the completed experiments in Illinois indicate that a $500 reemployment bonus paid to workers (but not to employers) has the effect of reducing the length of unemployment spells and associated UI outlays. Woodbury and Spiegelman (1987) calculate a benefit-cost ratio for the Claimant Bonus Experiment with the very favorable result that state regular UI benefit payments are reduced by $2.32 for each $1.00 of bonus payments made.

Preliminary findings of the New Jersey UI Reemployment Demonstration Project also provide evidence on the effectiveness of a reemployment bonus program as well as of JSA and retraining services. Corson and Kerachsky (1987) report that the JSA-only treatment reduces length of UI benefits by slightly over half a week and the amount of benefits by nearly $88. Adding the reemployment bonus to JSA services further decreases both length and amount of benefits. In view of the size of the average bonus payment (about $1,300), however, the incremental effect of the bonus program does not appear to be large enough to make this treatment cost effective.

Consistent with the results of the Texas WAD projects and the Downriver and Buffalo demonstrations, the New Jersey experiment indicates that the incremental impact of retraining (above that of JSA services only) on length and amount of UI benefits is essentially zero.

In interpreting this result, Corson and Kerachsky stress that their estimates are likely to understate the true impact of retraining since individuals enrolled in training programs continue to collect UI. The benefits of training in terms of reducing UI expenditures are thus expected to occur in the longer run as retrained workers enjoy more stable employment.

In summary, the available quantitative evidence strongly supports the inclusion of JSA in the spectrum of reemployment services that should be offered to displaced workers. The evidence is not nearly as strong concerning the net impact of training programs; and, given their relatively high cost, the cost effectiveness of retraining is open to question. Nevertheless, the authors of the evaluation reports reviewed are unanimous in cautioning that the impact of training programs may be understated in their empirical analyses.

Because of the limited number of quantitative evaluations available and the uncertainties in interpreting the results of those that do exist, particularly with respect to retraining, this study has devoted considerable attention to a "process analysis" of the initiatives examined. Rather than attempting to measure program outcomes, process analysis involves a qualitative evaluation of how well the program is operating. The operation of a particular program, in turn, is determined to a substantial extent by its design; and the discussion now turns to a consideration of several important design issues.

Question 3: How should particular adjustment assistance services be provided?

Chapter 2 introduced two related design issues involved in the provision of retraining services. The first of these concerns the use of performance-based contracting, and the second involves the extent of employer participation in reemployment programs. The main advantage of performance-based contracting is that program planners, once they have established their performance standards, can shift to training providers the burden of making sure that trainees acquire marketable skills. Performance-based contracting thus eliminates, at least for program planners, the necessity of forecasting the occupational demand for labor in order to select retraining curricula appropriately.

Among the state-level programs considered, California's Employment Training Panel program has gone the furthest in establishing stringent performance standards and in basing the reimbursement of training vendors solely on their performance in satisfactorily meeting these standards. As described in chapter 2, the Panel withholds the full negotiated payment per person until trainees have completed their training programs, are placed in training-related jobs at wage rates stipulated in the contract, and are retained in those jobs for at least 90 days.

An assessment of the California ETP program reveals, nonetheless, certain disadvantages of insisting on high performance standards. One of these is the incentive for training vendors to cream off the most able of those eligible for retraining assistance in order to satisfy placement rate requirements. A second disadvantage is that by withholding payment until after trainees have been placed in jobs for 90 days, external training providers such as community colleges and vocational-technical institutes may be discouraged from program participation (see Cyert and Mowery 1987:152). To the extent that educational institutions opt not to participate, Panel officials are restricted to employers for providing training; and employers have a natural incentive to seek program funding for the retraining of current employees. If in the absence of the program these employees would have been retrained anyway, there is no net increase in the delivery of training services and employers receive a windfall gain at the expense of taxpayers.

Although employers may serve as training providers in the ETP program, their broader role includes initiating the retraining process by requesting funding for a particular project. Once a project has received ETP approval, in addition, the employer determines criteria for selecting trainees, helps to select the curricula, and sets performance standards. In return, participating employers must make a good-faith commitment to hire program graduates. Tailoring retraining programs in this way clearly helps to solve the problem of workers being trained in skills not in demand. Moreover, tailored retraining is also important in meeting the twin goals of most states of encouraging economic development and reducing UI expenditures.

From a social perspective, the disavantages of tailored training programs, as noted, include creaming in the trainee-selection process and committing public funds to retraining individuals who might otherwise have been retrained at the employer's own expense. The discussion of the Minnesota Employment and Economic Development wage-subsidy program indicated that it is possible to take the opposite approach of targeting assistance to specific groups of hard-to-employ persons and still enjoy widespread business support. MEED offers employers who hire targeted workers a subsidy of up to $4 per hour in wages and up to $1 per hour in fringe benefits for a period not to exceed six months. In return, Minnesota employers agree to retain program participants on their payrolls for at least 12 months beyond the subsidy period. The support of the business community enjoyed by the MEED program is particularly interesting in view of unfavorable evidence from the Dayton wage-subsidy experiment showing that the placement rates of the two treatment groups are *lower* than the placement rate of the control group. Burtless' (1985) explanation for this unexpected result is that program vouchers were primarily viewed by employers as a signal of potentially poor job performance.

While chapter 2 emphasized that it is critical for a retraining program to enjoy the support of employers, chapters 3 and 4 brought out that employers' approval is equally important in the provision of other reemployment services. A case in point is the delivery of services at the site of facilities slated for a mass layoff or closure.

Question 4: What are the best time and place to provide assistance?

Most analysts take the position that reemployment assistance programs are most successful if they are located on-site and are in place before workers lose their jobs. Workers can be readily contacted at the workplace, and early adjustment assistance helps to avoid the discouragement and loss of self-respect that often goes along with an unexpected job loss. The involvement of employers in such on-site programs includes, at a minimum, supplying advance notice of planned layoffs and plant closures, making space available to program staff members within plant gates, and providing workers time off to attend presentations detailing available services.

Beginning with the issue of advance notification, chapter 4 provided an overview of mandatory advance notice laws on the books in three states, federal plant closing regulation enacted in the Worker Adjustment and Retraining Notification Act of 1988, and the limited empirical evidence currently available on the effect of notification on length of unemployment spells and subsequent earnings upon reemployment. Although the empirical evidence discussed is subject to a number of qualifications, it does seem to indicate that advance notice is effective in speeding up the transition of displaced workers to new jobs, primarily by encouraging workers to locate employment prior to scheduled termination dates. Thus advance notice appears to reduce both the private and social costs of adjustment associated with worker displacement.

What makes mandatory advance notice legislation controversial is the question of whether the benefit to workers and to society as a whole is sufficient to offset the private costs to employers. These private costs include increased inflexibility in adjusting workforce size and a possible negative effect on worker productivity. The inflexibility argument is usually made by associating the much slower rate of employment growth in Western Europe than in the U.S. since 1970 to restrictions many European countries place on firms' ability to carry out layoffs. Whatever the merits of this argument, it should be noted that the failure of employers to provide advance notice imposes costs (or "externalities") on workers and communities that are not shared by the firms making the layoffs. Regarding the impact on labor productivity, what evidence is available does not support the argument that productivity is adversely affected during the period of notification.

The most common on-site assistance program in this country takes the form of rapid-response teams. As implemented by various states, employer involvement in rapid-response team programs ranges from a minimum level of cooperation (i.e., giving advance notice, providing space, and offering workers time off) to active participation in helping to place workers in new jobs. At the extreme of minimal employer involvement, the rapid-response team consists of representatives of relevant state agencies; team members make on-site presentations to affected workers on the details of registering for UI benefits, requirements for continued UI eligibility, and available ES and Title III JTPA retraining and job search assistance services.

At the other extreme of employer involvement, the model usually pointed to is the Canadian Industrial Adjustment Service program. The thrust of the IAS is to encourage the employer and, where present, the union or unions representing the displaced workers to utilize their informal labor market contacts to place workers in suitable job openings. Placement rather than retraining, relocation, or counseling is emphasized. The primary role of the IAS is a limited one of securing from the parties a commitment of time and financial resources in the formation of a joint labor-management adjustment committee. It is the adjustment committee's job to organize and put into effect the placement process. Worth noting in the recent report of the Secretary of Labor's Task Force on Economic Adjustment and Worker Dislocation (1986:28–33) is the recommendation that state-level Displaced Worker Units be formed to play an IAS-like role in mobilizing the resources of labor and management to respond rapidly to worker displacement.

An important advantage of on-site adjustment assistance is that programs can be appropriately targeted to workers displaced by a plant closing or permanent layoff. As noted earlier in this chapter, however, the ripple effect of the closing of a large plant will generate additional displacement among employees of suppliers to the closed plant and local retail and service outlets. The question then arises whether workers displaced by the secondary effects of a plant closure can be distinguished from other unemployed workers in the local labor market. From a policy perspective, the answer to this question is important to avoid providing reemployment services to unemployed workers expected to experience little difficulty in finding new jobs or likely to return to their previous employers.

Chapter 3 pointed out that one of the two main objectives of the New Jersey UI Reemployment Demonstration is to determine whether it is possible to identify by the fifth week of the claim period unemployed workers who are likely to exhaust UI benefits but are unlikely to return to their old or similar jobs. (The other main objective, as noted earlier, is to measure the effectiveness of alternative reemployment services, including the reemployment bonus.) The methodological approach taken in the demonstration is to screen UI claimants using five eligibility requirements, the most important of which are three years of tenure with the pre-UI employer and absence of a definite recall date. Preliminary results provided by Corson and Kerachsky (1987) indicate that the five screens do seem to restrict the demonstration-eligible population to persons whose attributes are usually associated with displaced workers and reemployment difficulty. Nevertheless, the eligible population is also found to include claimants previously employed in growing sectors of the economy, such as the service industry, as well as claimants who eventually returned to their former employers.

Question 5: Is there a role for initiatives designed to keep existing plants open?

In the case of a plant closing or mass layoff, most of the initiatives discussed in this monograph are designed to ease the adjustment of laid-off workers into jobs with new employers. The main question raised in chapter 5, in contrast, is the appropriateness of policy intervention to enable existing firms or plants to remain open in local labor markets that are sufficiently depressed that alternative employment opportunities are limited to low-wage jobs offering little potential for advancement. Possible forms of intervention are (1) assistance to allow current owners to continue operating or to attract new owners from outside the firm, (2) assistance to encourage employee buyouts of existing facilities, and (3) assistance to enable displaced workers to start up their own small businesses. Unfortunately, the available evidence on these categories of assistance is limited to a handful of qualitative studies.

Assistance to current or new owners of established facilities is commonly embodied in "enterprise zone" programs, and 21 states have passed some form of enterprise zone legislation. The basic idea underlying enterprise zones is to target special opportunities and benefits to firms and residents of distressed areas within the state (including blighted inner-city neighborhoods). As originally conceived, the enterprise zone was envisioned as a tool to stimulate economic development by lifting the twin burdens of government regulation and high tax rates, both of which serve to reduce individual work effort and entrepreneurial initiative.

As described by Bendick and Rasmussen (1986), however, state enterprise zone laws have little to do with creating islands of unfettered free enterprise. Rather, the major features of zone programs are (1) a reduction in total tax burdens, as opposed to reduced marginal tax rates, and (2) extensive government activity within zones. The latter feature includes such activities as land-use planning, infrastructure development, improvements in public services, provision of loans and technical assistance to businesses, and training programs directed toward disadvantaged workers. The high level of government activity within zones often imposes on businessmen excessively burdensome red tape and operating requirements as conditions for receiving benefits. Bendick and Rasmussen (1986:118–19) note that a number of states are likely soon to revise their legislation, and that future zone programs will probably reflect a greater awareness of the needs of small and indigenous firms, as opposed to those of large in-migrants. Key problems generally thought to adversely affect the survival of small businesses are lack of access to affordable financing, lack of experience in running a business, and lack of predictable demand for the goods or services produced. State support to small business incubator programs represents one approach to dealing with the first and second of these problems.

Turning to the topic of employee buyouts, about one-third of the states have on their books legislation specifically promoting employee ownership of troubled enterprises. The interest of policymakers in employee-ownership initiatives appears to stem largely from two factors: (1) the series of tax incentives embodied in Employee Stock Ownership Plans (ESOPs), and (2) reports of a favorable impact on labor productivity and profits of giving workers a stake in their companies and participation in decisionmaking. Case studies of particular companies (e.g., Weirton Steel) suggest that employee buyout programs may indeed increase labor productivity to an extent permitting the survival of firms that would otherwise have closed. Surveys carried out by the National Center for Employee Ownership also indicate that ESOP firms exhibit faster sales and employment growth than conventional firms.

Nevertheless, current discussions of ESOPs emphasize their role as a low-cost strategy used by existing managements to finance corporate restructurings and to fend off corporate raiders. Relatively uncommon is the use of ESOPs to save jobs that would otherwise be lost to plant closings. In addition, employee ownership is often found to involve little participation in decisionmaking; and employees shoulder increased risk in those cases in which company stock is substituted for diversified savings and pension plans. It seems reasonable to conclude, as do Rosen, Klein, and Young (1986), that ESOPs can operate to motivate workers and increase job satisfaction only if employers are (1) willing to make significant financial contributions to the plan, (2) strongly committed to the philosophy of employee ownership, and (3) ready to develop an active program to educate employees about the ESOP.

Although programs to assist unemployed workers to become self-employed have yet to be implemented in this country, both state and federal policymakers are currently exhibiting a strong interest in the unemployed entrepreneur concept. Accounting for this interest is evidence showing that small firms contribute disproportionately to creating new jobs, and that many independent small businesses are successful attempts at self-employment. Also important is the belief of program advocates that many displaced workers possess marketable skills and entrepreneurial talent that can be effectively utilized in their own small businesses once they have received assistance in getting started.

Several European countries have established programs that provide financial and limited training assistance to would-be entrepreneurs. The best known of these initiatives are the French Unemployed Entrepreneurs Program and the British Enterprise Allowance Scheme. While the French program provides participants with a lump-sum payment, the British program supplies monthly payments for a maximum of 52 weeks. Both programs are currently funded by general tax revenues. In France, however, funding was obtained prior to April 1984 from the unemployment insurance trust fund.

Although neither the French nor the British program has been subjected to a formal evaluation involving a control group comparison, recent studies of the two programs by Bendick and Egan (1987) and the USDOL (1986) are helpful in assessing the potential of the unemployed entrepreneur concept for returning the unemployed to work and creating additional jobs. Both studies reach pessimistic conclusions. The major concerns about the concept are threefold. The first is the question of whether new businesses started by program participants would have taken place in the absence of the program. If the answer is "yes," participants receive a windfall gain at the expense of taxpayers. The available evidence suggests that about 50 percent of British program participants would have set up their businesses without program assistance.

A second concern is the possibility that subsidized firms will compete against and possibly displace existing firms in the same local product markets. British government estimates reported by Bendick and Egan (1987:535) suggest that because of displacement, about one worker is thrown into unemployment for every two workers employed. It might be noted parenthetically that the problem of displacement exists for all of the initiatives examined in this study, and even the random-assignment experiments that have been carried out shed little or no light on the severity of the problem.

Finally, there is a concern about how many new jobs self-employment programs would actually generate. The USDOL report (1986:63) suggests that subsidies to encourage start-ups by unemployed workers with no previous entrepreneurial experience and little initial capital to invest may exacerbate already high rates of small business failure. In addition, Bendick and Egan (1987:536–37) indicate for both the British and French programs that only a small subset of subsidized firms surviving three years are likely to provide employment opportunities in addition to the job held by the proprietor.

Adding to the uncertainty about the wisdom of implementing the unemployed entrepreneur concept in this country is experience provided by the Entrepreneurial Training Pilot Project carried out in Ohio in 1985–86. This small-scale project used JTPA Title III funds to supply self-employment training to 200 displaced workers. In their evaluation of the project, Mangum and Tansky (1987) conclude that entrepreneurial training is likely to result in viable small businesses only for those displaced workers with the rare combination of substantial savings or equity in their homes, prior management experience obtained from previous jobs, and a relatively short period of joblessness.

Question 6: How should reemployment asistance to displaced workers be funded?

Most of the state-level displaced worker programs examined in this study are funded by state general tax revenues. The main alternative source of funding is state UI trust funds. At present, however, federal UI regulations prohibit the use of trust funds for purposes other than providing workers a partial replacement of earnings during short spells of involuntary unemployment. To be eligible for UI income-maintenance benefits, unemployed workers must meet a ''work test;'' that is, they must be available for and actively seeking employment. The one case in which the work test is waived is when a UI claimant is enrolled in a training program approved by the state's employment security agency. States are prohibited from using trust funds to pay directly for the costs of training.

The underlying premise of the present UI system is that unemployment is basically a temporary experience best dealt with by maintaining workers' incomes while they engage in job search or wait to be recalled. Critics of restricting the use of UI trust funds to income-maintenance benefits argue, however, that the main reemployment problem faced by many displaced workers is not one of riding out a temporary spell of unemployment until a cyclical upturn occurs. These critics suggest, rather, that what is needed is labor market adjustment assistance initiatives including retraining to qualify workers for vacant jobs and programs to subsidize reemployment. The implication that follows is that UI trust funds should be opened up to fund innovative programs which are aimed more directly at solving fundamental problems hindering the reemployment of displaced workers.

As an additional indication of the inadequacy of the present UI system, critics point out that UI benefits are reaching a diminishing percentage of the jobless. Burtless (1983) reports that the fraction of unemployed workers receiving regular, extended, and supplemental UI benefits was lower in the 1981–82 recession than in any other postwar recession.

The possibility of using UI trust funds to pay for adjustment assistance programs has been considered at two places in this monograph. In chapter 2, the pioneering approach of California to diverting a small part of regular UI tax revenues to finance its ETP program was examined. A surplus in California's trust fund permitted the state's legislature in 1983 to create an earmarked fund financed by a 0.1 percent payroll tax, while at the same time employers were given a 0.1 percent reduction in their regular UI tax rates. Delaware and Washington state have subsequently funded permanent retraining and job search assistance programs using the diversion approach.

The second mention of an alternative use of UI trust funds occurred in chapter 5 in connection with the funding of unemployed entrepreneur initiatives. Advocates of this concept argue that rather than offering a subsidy not to work, UI trust funds could be put to better use by supplying an incentive for the unemployed to use their skills and entrepreneurial talent to create jobs for themselves and for others.

It should be emphasized, nevertheless, that the present policy restricting the use of UI trust funds has many adherents. Organized labor and a number of business organizations have consistently taken the position that UI trust funds should continue to be used only to fund temporary income-maintenance benefits. There are two main arguments supporting this position. The first is based on the issue of trust fund solvency, and the second involves conformity to the basic insurance principles underlying the financing of the UI system. To anticipate the discussion that follows, these two arguments appear to carry sufficient weight that any basic departure from the current concept of unemployment insurance should be approached cautiously.

As noted in chapter 1, the UI system has served for over 50 years as the first line of defense against temporary income losses due to unemployment. Advocates of the present system express concern that should UI trust funds be opened up to fund alternative initiatives, the ability of the system to provide traditional income-maintenance benefits would be jeopardized. Vroman (1986) documents the series of recessions from 1970 through the early 1980s that severely depleted the trust funds of a number of states, causing them to borrow heavily from the federal government. Many of these states have been able to reduce their indebtedness during the improved economic climate of the mid-1980s. From an actuarial perspective, nevertheless, the condition of the UI system is still weak; and the onset of a new recession would be likely to trigger a repetition of heavy borrowing and debt accumulation.

An assessment of just how much of a drain adjustment assistance initiatives would impose on trust fund balances is difficult for two reasons. The first is the uncertainty regarding the longer-run effectiveness of these initiatives. In principle, short-run trust fund withdrawals might be more than offset by longer-run inflows as the initiatives pay off in a workforce that is less susceptible to unemployment. The available evidence, however, provides very little insight into the likely trade-off between initial costs and longer-term benefits.

The second reason, as discussed earlier in this chapter, is that displaced workers are not easily distinguished from workers unemployed for frictional, seasonal, or cyclical reasons. Thus there is considerable uncertainty as to the number of unemployed workers who should be counted as displaced from their jobs at any particular point in time. This uncertainty is important because it is displaced workers who are expected to benefit from alternative forms of labor market adjustment asistance, while short-term income maintenance is more appropriate for other categories of the unemployed. Excessive costs are incurred if services are provided to unemployed workers who will get their former jobs back or who can easily locate new jobs when the economy recovers. Such excessive costs threaten the ability of the UI system to supply traditional wage-replacement benefits, particularly during recessions. On the other hand, a significant equity problem is raised by the denial of alternative services to individuals who would benefit from them but who do not happen to satisfy a particular displaced worker definition.

Next consider the insurance-based argument for remaining faithful to the present policy of restricting the use of UI trust funds. To understand this argument, it should first be emphasized that the UI system is intended to be fully self-financing by a payroll tax imposed on employers. The underlying philosophy of this method of financing is that the individual employer has a responsibility for former employees. It is this philosophy that gives the program its insurance character. Employers are assessed insurance "premiums" in the form of payroll taxes, which are used to create state trust funds. Covered employees who have been laid off are then eligible to draw on these funds. States are free to determine the payroll taxes they assess; and tax rate schedules are said to be "experienced rated," which simply means that tax rates vary depending on the employer's layoff rates and on the fraction of former employees receiving benefits. The "moral hazard" problem associated with the incentive for insured individuals to decide on a course of action that makes them eligible for insurance benefits is dealt with by restricting UI payments to workers who are involuntarily unemployed and by providing a relatively low replacement rate for lost earnings.

Hansen and Byers (1986) observe that the payment of income-maintenance benefits to workers enrolled in training programs represents a significant weakening of the insurance philosophy underpinning the UI system because these workers are not actively seeking employment. The essential point is that the UI system was designed to provide a *minimum* number of weekly benefit checks necessary to find a job by ensuring that eligible unemployed workers will act in their own self-interest to end their unemployment. The present practice of waiving the work test for claimants undergoing retraining implies receipt of a fixed stream of benefits depending on the length of the program. Since eligible workers may have some choice among retraining options, they are in effect being given a "right" or "entitlement" to receive the *maximum* number of payments allowable under state law. Trust fund financing of adjustment assistance initiatives including directly paying the cost of training programs, wage subsidies, and unemployed entrepreneur programs clearly has the impact of expanding worker choice, thereby further undermining the philosophical basis of the system. With the experience rating of UI taxes, an additional equity issue that arises is whether it is still reasonable to expect employers in declining industries to subsidize the retraining or reemployment of workers who will more than likely locate jobs in the industries that are expanding.

Among the reemployment initiatives described in this study, JSA is the one that is conceptually most consistent with the objective of providing assistance for only the minimum period of time necessary to find a job. Moreover, the available empirical evidence summarized earlier strongly indicates that JSA programs reduce the length of unemployment spells. The results of the Illinois experiments also suggest that the reemployment bonus concept offers considerable promise in terms of stimulating the intensity of job search effort.

An Ideal Adjustment Assistance System

Drawing on the discussion of the six policy questions just considered, a final issue that remains to be dealt with involves the ideal mix of adjustment assistance services to meet the needs of displaced workers. The point that comes out most strongly from the discussion is that JSA should be the core service provided in the ideal system. JSA has been shown empirically to be effective in speeding up the reemployment process, it allows for quick intervention before workers disperse after layoffs or plant closings, and it is relatively cheap. In view of the practical difficulties of distinguishing displaced workers from other unemployed workers, the low cost of JSA services is particularly attractive because it makes it feasible to supply assistance even to those unemployed workers who turn out *ex post* to have little difficulty in locating new jobs or are recalled to their old jobs.

The roles of retraining and remedial education programs are not as clear cut. Vocational training programs are substantially more expensive than JSA, and the empirical evidence summarized here indicates that retraining has little or no impact on labor market outcomes as typically measured. However, there is an important caveat to consider with respect to this evidence. This is the issue of whether the training programs examined provided workers with skills that were appropriate to their backgrounds and interests and at the same time were salable in the marketplace. Process analyses of the California ETP program suggest that direct employer involvement in the training process is critical in supplying marketable skills, and Minnesota's MEED program indicates that employer support can be enlisted even for programs targeted to hard-to-employ persons. It seems reasonable to conclude, along with Bloom and Kulik (1986:181), that in the ideal system skill training should be offered sparingly for well-specified needs and only where adequate local training resources are present.

Most analysts agree that at least 20 percent of the displaced worker population is seriously deficient in basic reading and problem-solving skills. As noted earlier in this chapter, remedial education has received little attention in this study because of the emphasis of most states on economic development rather than human capital investment. Nevertheless, a typical finding in the empirical literature is that displaced workers with low levels of formal education are much more likely than other displaced workers to experience lengthy spells of unemployment and low earnings upon reemployment. In other words, these are precisely the displaced workers who should be targeted for assistance. Remedial education thus appears to be an essential service to be offered to the minority of displaced workers determined in the assessment and testing phase of JSA programs to lack basic skills.

At the present time, there is simply not enough information available to justify including in the ideal system initiatives offering direct assistance to employers in order to retain or replace jobs. The three categories of employer-assistance programs examined in this study involved aid to current owners to stay in business, employee buyout assistance, and aid to unemployed workers to start up their own small businesses. Perhaps the best qualitative evidence on the effectiveness of these programs is available for unemployed entrepreneur programs. This evidence suggests quite strongly that the individuals most likely to create and operate a viable small business successfully possess personal attributes that exclude them from the minority of displaced workers who face the most severe adjustment problems.

REFERENCES

Abraham, Katharine G., and Susan N. Houseman. "Employment and Hours Adjustment: A U.S./German Comparison." Department of Economics, University of Maryland (April 1988).

Addison, John T. "The Controversy Over Advance Notice Legislation in the United States." Department of Economics, University of South Carolina (January 1988).

Addison, John T., and Pedro Portugal. "Job Displacement, Relative Wage Changes and Duration of Unemployment." Department of Economics, University of South Carolina (August 1987a).

_____ and _____. "The Effect of Advance Notification of Plant Closings on Unemployment," *Industrial and Labor Relations Review* 41 (October 1987b): 3–16.

Arthur Young. "Study of the California Employment Training Panel." May 1985.

Balderston, Kris M. "Plant Closings, Layoffs, and Worker Readjustment: The States' Response to Economic Change." National Governors' Association (July 1986).

Baldwin, Stephen E. "Trade Adjustment Assistance: Part of the Solution, or Part of the Problem?" National Commission for Employment Policy (February 1987).

Barnow, Burt S. "The Impact of CETA Programs on Earnings: A Review of the Literature," *Journal of Human Resources* 22 (Spring 1987): 157–93.

Bendick, Marc, and Mary Lou Egan. "Transfer Payment Diversion for Small Business Development: British and French Experience," *Industrial and Labor Relations Review* 40 (July 1987): 528–42.

Bendick, Marc, and David W. Rasmussen. "Enterprise Zones and Inner-City Economic Revitalization." In *Reagan and the Cities,* edited by George E. Peterson and Carol W. Lewis, 97–129. Washington, D.C.: Urban Institute Press, 1986.

Bhagwati, Jagdish. "Veto Trade Bill, but for Right Reasons," *The Wall Street Journal* (April 22, 1988): 22.

Birch, David L. "Who Creates Jobs?" *The Public Interest* 65 (Fall 1981): 3–14.

Bloom, Howard S. "Lessons From the Delaware Dislocated Worker Pilot Program," *Evaluation Review* 11 (April 1987): 157–77.

Bloom, Howard S., and Jane Kulik. "Evaluation of the Worker Adjustment Demonstration: Final Report." Abt Associates (July 1986).

Bluestone, Barry, and Bennett Harrison. *The Deindustrialization of America.* New York: Basic Books, 1982.

158

Blumenthal, Karen. "Off Target? Job-Training Effort, Critics Say Fails Many Who Need It Most," *The Wall Street Journal* (February 9, 1987): 1, 16.

Burgess, Paul L., and Jerry L. Kingston. *An Incentives Approach to Improving the Unemployment Compensation System.* Kalamazoo, MI: W.E. Upjohn Institute, 1987.

Burtless, Gary. "Why Is Insured Unemployment So Low?" *Brookings Papers on Economic Activity* (1983): 225–49.

_____. "Are Targeted Wage Subsidies Harmful? Evidence from a Wage Voucher Experiment," *Industrial and Labor Relations Review* 39 (October 1985): 105–14.

Burtless, Gary, and Larry L. Orr. "Are Classical Experiments Needed for Manpower Policy?" *Journal of Human Resources* 21 (Fall 1986): 606–39.

BusinessWeek. "There Really Are Jobs After Retraining." January 28, 1985.

Choate, Pat, and Dennis C. Carey. "An IRA for Structural Unemployment," *Challenge* (November–December 1985): 57–59.

Cook, Robert F., ed. *Worker Dislocation: Case Studies of Causes and Cures.* Kalamazoo, MI: W.E. Upjohn Institute, 1987.

Corson, Walter, Rebecca Maynard, and Jack Wichita. "Process and Implementation Issues In the Design and Conduct of Programs to Aid the Reemployment of Dislocated Workers." Mathematica Policy Research (October 30, 1984).

Corson, Walter, David Long, and Walter Nicholson. "Evaluation of the Charleston Claimant Placement and Work Test Demonstration." Unemployment Insurance Occasional Paper 85-2, U.S. Department of Labor, Employment and Training Administration (1985).

Corson, Walter, Sharon Long, and Rebecca Maynard. "An Impact Evaluation of the Buffalo Dislocated Worker Demonstration Program." Mathematica Policy Research (March 12, 1985).

Corson, Walter, and Stuart Kerachsky. "The New Jersey Unemployment Insurance Reemployment Demonstration Project: Interim Report." U.S. Department of Labor, Employment and Training Administration (1987).

Cyert, Richard M., and David C. Mowery, eds. *Technology and Employment: Innovation and Growth in the U.S. Economy.* Washington, D.C.: National Academy Press, 1987.

Division of Employment Security, Commonwealth of Massachusetts. "A Report to the Legislature on Worker Assistance Programs under the Mature Industries Law." February 1987.

Drouin, Marie-Josee. "Europe's Jobless Owe It to the 'Ins'," *The Wall Street Journal* (December 12, 1986).

Ehrenberg, Ronald G., and George H. Jakubson. *Advance Notice Provisions in Plant Closing Legislation.* Kalamazoo, MI: W.E. Upjohn Institute, 1988.

Employment Training Panel (ETP). *Annual Report.* September 30, 1984.

————. *Annual Report.* 1985.

————. *Report to the Legislature.* November 1986.

————. *Report to the Legislature 1987.*

Fedrau, Ruth H. "Responses to Plant Closures and Major Reductions in Force: Private Sector and Community-based Models," *The Annals of the American Academy of Political and Social Science* 475 (September 1984): 80–95.

Feldstein, Martin. "Unemployment Compensation: Adverse Incentives and Distributional Anomalies," *National Tax Journal* 27 (June 1974): 231–44.

Flaim, Paul O., and Ellen Sehgel. "Displaced Workers of 1979–83: How Well Have They Fared?" *Monthly Labor Review* 108 (June 1985): 3–16.

Folbre, Nancy R., Julia L. Leighton, and Melissa R. Roderick. "Plant Closings and Their Regulation in Maine, 1971–1982," *Industrial and Labor Relations Review* 37 (January 1984): 185–96.

Fraker, Thomas, and Rebecca Maynard. "The Adequacy of Comparison Group Designs for Evaluations of Employment-Related Programs," *Journal of Human Resources* 22 (Spring 1987): 194–227.

Galante, Steven P. "One Solution for the Jobless: Make Them Business Owners," *The Wall Street Journal* (November 30, 1987): 21.

Gupta, Udayan. "States Play Expanding Role In Funding Technology Firms," *The Wall Street Journal* (November 11, 1987): 27.

Hall, Arden R. "The Counseling and Wage Subsidy Treatments," *Journal of Human Resources* 15 (Fall 1980): 591–610.

Hamermesh, Daniel S. *Jobless Pay and the Economy.* Baltimore: Johns Hopkins University Press, 1977.

————. "The Cost of Worker Displacement," *Quarterly Journal of Economics* 102 (February 1987): 51–75.

————. "What Do We Know About Worker Displacement in the U.S.?" *Industrial Relations* 28 (Winter 1989): 51–59.

Hamermesh, Daniel S., Joseph J. Cordes, and Robert S. Goldfarb. "Compensating Displaced Workers—What, How Much, How?" In *Labor Market Adjustments in the Pacific Basin,* edited by Peter T. Chinloy and Ernst W. Stromsdorfer, 243–65. Boston: Klewer-Niuhoff, 1987.

Hammer, Tove H., and Robert N. Stern. "A Yo-Yo Model of Cooperation: Union Participation in Management at the Rath Packing Company," *Industrial and Labor Relations Review* 39 (April 1986): 337–49.

160

Hansen, W. Lee, and James F. Byers. "Unemployment Compensation and Retraining: Can a Closer Link Be Forged?" Paper presented at the conference, "Unemployment Compensation : The Second Half-Century." Racine, WI, February 20–22, 1986.

Heckman, James J., V. Joseph Hotz, and Marcelo Dabos. "Do We Need Experimental Data to Evaluate the Impact of Manpower Training on Earnings?" *Evaluation Review* 11 (August 1987): 395–427.

Horvath, Francis W. "The Pulse of Economic Change: Displaced Workers of 1981–85," *Monthly Labor Review* 110 (July 1987): 3–12.

Howland, Marie. *Plant Closings and Worker Displacement: The Regional Issues.* Kalamazoo, MI: W.E. Upjohn Institute, 1988.

Jaggers, Meredith, John Herrem, Mary Witt, and Elizabeth Blessinger. "Wisconsin Job Service ERP Pilot Project: Final Report." Wisconsin Department of Industry, Labor, and Human Relations (December 1984).

Jones, Derek C. "The Productivity Effects of Worker Directors and Financial Participation in the Firm: The Case of British Retail Cooperatives," *Industrial and Labor Relations Review* 41 (October 1987): 79–92.

Jones, Derek C., and Jan Svejnar. "Participation, Profit Sharing, Worker Ownership and Efficiency in Italian Producer Cooperatives," *Economica* 52 (November 1985): 449–65.

Kingston, Jerry L., Paul L. Burgess, and Robert D. St. Louis. "Unemployment Insurance Overpayments: Evidence and Implications," *Industrial and Labor Relations Review* 39 (April 1986): 323–36.

Kotlowitz, Alex, and Ed Bean. "Spate of Corporate Buy-Outs by ESOPs Raises Questions of Benefits to Workers," *The Wall Street Journal* (September 30, 1987): 14.

Kulik, Jane, D. Alton Smith, and Ernst W. Stromsdorfer. "The Downriver Community Conference Economic Readjustment Program: Final Evaluation Report." Abt Associates (May 18, 1984).

Kuttner, Robert. "Blue-Collar Boardrooms," *The New Republic* (June 17, 1985a): 18–23.

————. "Getting Off the Dole," *The Atlantic Monthly* (September 1985b): 74–79.

LaLonde, Robert J. "Evaluating the Econometric Evaluations of Training Programs with Experimental Data," *American Economic Review* 76 (September 1986): 604–20.

Lazear, Edward P. "Job-Security Rules Cut Employment in Much of Europe," *The Wall Street Journal* (October 14, 1987): 32.

Levitan, Sar A., and Frank Gallo. *A Second Chance: Training for Jobs.* Kalamazoo, MI: W.E. Upjohn Institute, 1988.

Lovell, Malcolm R., Jr. "An Antidote for Protectionism," *The Brookings Review* 3 (Fall 1984): 23–28.

Madden, Janice F. "Gender Differences in the Cost of Displacement: An Empirical Test of Discrimination in the Labor Market," *American Economic Review* 77 (May 1987): 246–51.

_____. "The Distribution of Economic Losses Among Displaced Workers: Measurement Methods Matter," *Journal of Human Resources* 23 (Winter 1988): 93–107.

Mangum, Stephen L., and Judy Tansky. "Self Employment Training as an Intervention Strategy for Displaced or Disadvantaged Workers." Faculty of Management and Human Resources, Ohio State University (December 1987).

Miller, James P. "Joining the Game: Some Workers Set Up LBOs of Their Own and Benefit Greatly," *The Wall Street Journal* (December 12, 1988): A1, A4.

Minnesota Department of Jobs and Training. *Minnesota Employment and Economic Development (MEED) Wage Subsidy Program, July 1985–December 1986.* 1987.

Moffitt, Robert, and Walter Nicholson. "The Effect of Unemployment Insurance on Unemployment: The Case of Federal Supplemental Benefits," *Review of Economic and Statistics* 64 (February 1982): 1–11.

Moore, Richard W., Wellford W. Wilms, and Roger E. Bolus. "Training for Change: An Analysis of the Outcomes of California Employment Training Panel Programs." Training Research Corporation (January 19, 1988).

Nelson, Richard R. "State Labor Legislation Enacted in 1983," *Monthly Labor Review* 107 (January 1984): 59–75.

_____. "State Labor Legislation Enacted in 1984," *Monthly Labor Review* 108 (January 1985): 27–42.

_____. "State Labor Legislation Enacted in 1985," *Monthly Labor Review* 109 (January 1986): 34–54.

_____. "State Labor Legislation Enacted in 1986," *Monthly Labor Review* 110 (January 1987): 49–66.

O'Boyle, Thomas F., and Terence Roth. "War and Peace: Labor Relations Vary at Two Steelmakers; So Do Firms' Fortunes," *The Wall Street Journal* (September 17, 1985).

Office of Technology Assessment. *Technology and Structural Unemployment: Reemploying Displaced Adults.* Washington, D.C.: Congress of the United States, 1986.

Podgursky, Michael, and Paul Swaim. "Health Insurance Loss: The Case of the Displaced Worker," *Monthly Labor Review* 110 (April 1987a): 30–33.

_____ and _____. "Job Displacement and Earnings Loss: Evidence from the Displaced Worker Survey," *Industrial and Labor Relations Review* 41 (October 1987b): 17–29.

———— and ————. "Duration of Joblessness Following Displacement," *Industrial Relations* 26 (Fall 1987c): 213–26.

Rangan, Asha. "MEED Works: A Look at Minnesota's Investment In People, Jobs and Communities." The Jobs Now Coalition (March 1985).

Rode, Peter. "MEED Means *More* Business: Job Growth through Minnesota's Wage Subsidy Program." The Jobs Now Coalition (March 1988).

Rosen, Corey M., and Katherine J. Klein. "Job-Creating Performance of Employee-Owned Firms," *Monthly Labor Review* 106 (August 1983): 15–19.

Rosen, Corey M., Katherine J. Klein, and Karen M. Young. *Employee Ownership in America: The Equity Solution.* Lexington, MA: D.C. Heath, 1986.

Salzman, Jeffrey D. "The Canadian-American Plant Closing Demonstration Project," *Compensation and Benefits Management* 3 (Summer 1987): 233–39.

Secretary of Labor's Task Force on Economic Adjustment and Worker Dislocation. "Economic Adjustment and Worker Dislocation in a Competitive Society." Washington, D.C. (December 1986).

St. Louis, Robert D., Paul L. Burgess, and Jerry L. Kingston. "Reported vs. Actual Job Search by Unemployment Insurance Claimants," *Journal of Human Resources* 21 (Winter 1986): 92–117.

Stevens, David. "State Industry-Specific Training Programs: 1986." University of Missouri-Columbia (December 1986).

Stone, Charles F., and Isabel V. Sawhill. "Trade's Impact on U.S. Jobs," *Challenge* (September–October 1987): 12–18.

Summers, Lawrence H. "Why Is the Unemployment Rate So Very High near Full Employment?" *Brookings Papers on Economic Activity* (1986): 339–83.

Swaim, Paul, and Michael Podgursky. "Advance Notice and Job Search: The Value of an Early Start." Department of Economics, University of Massachusetts at Amherst (June 1988).

Thornburgh, Richard. "The Pennsylvania Experience," *Economic Development Commentary* 12 (Spring 1988): 3–6.

Trolin, Brenda, and Sharon O. Randall. "Re-employing Unemployment Funds," *State Legislatures,* National Conference of State Legislatures (August 1987): 10–13.

Unemployment Insurance Service. "The New Jersey Unemployment Insurance Reemployment Demonstration Project: A Description." U.S. Department of Labor, Employment and Training Administration (May 14, 1986).

U.S. Department of Labor. "Alternative Uses of Unemployment Insurance." Employment and Training Administration (March 17, 1986).

U.S. General Accounting Office. "Dislocated Workers: Local Programs and Outcomes Under the Job Training Partnership Act." March 1987a.

————. "Plant Closings: Limited Advance Notice and Assistance Provided Dislocated Workers." July 1987b.

Vroman, Wayne. *The Funding Crisis in State Unemployment Insurance.* Kalamazoo, MI: W.E. Upjohn Institute, 1986.

Washington State Employment Security Department. "Special Employment Assistance Legislative Report." January 1987.

Weber, Arnold R., and David P. Taylor. "Procedures for Employee Displacement: Advance Notice of Plant Shutdown," *Journal of Business* 36 (July 1963): 302–15.

Weiner, Stuart E. "Enterprise Zones as a Means of Reducing Structural Unemployment," *Economic Review,* Federal Reserve Bank of Kansas City (March 1984): 3–16.

Wessel, David, and Buck Brown. "The Hyping of Small-Firm Job Growth," *The Wall Street Journal* (November 8, 1988): B1.

White, Joseph B. "Workers' Revenge: Factory Towns Start to Fight Back Angrily When Firms Pull Out," *The Wall Street Journal* (March 8, 1988): 1, 26.

Woodbury, Stephen A., and Robert G. Spiegelman. "Bonuses to Workers and Employers to Reduce Unemployment: Randomized Trials in Illinois," *American Economic Review* 77 (September 1987): 513–30.

INDEX